Rigoniworks

This novel is a work of fiction. Any reference to real people, events, establishments, organizations, or locales are intended only to give the fiction a sense of reality and authenticity, and are used fictitiously. All other names, characters, and places, and all dialogue and incidents portrayed in this book are the product of the author's imagination.

Time Once Again: Evolution of the Spirit.

Copyright © 2011 by James c. Rigoni / Rigoniworks.

Cover photo by James c. Rigoni

All rights reserved Printed in the United States of America. No part of this book may be used or reproduced in any manner whatsoever without written permission except in the case of a brief quotations embodied in critical articles and reviews. For book purchasing information and other photos: www.rigoniworks.com

First published in 2010 by Rigoniworks ®

Dedication

I dedicate this book to my Mom who is in Wisconsin, and my Dad who has moved on to another plane, for never telling me that my dreams were unattainable... If it weren't for that fact, this book may have never been written. I'm glad I picked them for my lessons this time around.

Acknowledgments

First, I'd like to thank you, the reader... I believe you have found my book for a reason. I share with you my truths and hope I have done my job in providing what it is you need, and also to have entertained you in the process.

I admit I've always skimmed past the *"thank-you's"* when I've picked up books, but now I realize just how important these people are to the writer. Many people have contributed to this book, some merely by telling me that it couldn't be done. But there are several people who stand out, and I believe were sent to me, providing their positive input and encouragement. A special thanks goes out to Mary Horn for telling me I had to find my voice and rewrite my story... after I had already written it once. Sally Wheelock for her words of wisdom and editing skills. Anne Franz for her input, insights, editing and especially for taking the time to read my written words out loud to me so I could hear my dream take on its own reality!!

Time Once Again
Evolution of the Spirit

A Novel

by

James c. Rigoni

Chapter 1
The Abyss

The gentle rocking motion was Jim's first clue that he wasn't going to find himself lying in his comfortable bed. He was reluctant to open his eyes, but rather than continue living in his denial, he opted to simply open them and face reality. When he did, he found himself exactly where he assumed he would be... Lying on his back in a little yellow inflatable boat, afloat in a place he could only describe as *different*... *different* in a Twilight Zone-ish sort of sense. He lay in a visceral environment of deep, rich aquamarine iridescence; an environment without a horizon or any other point of spatial reference. It was as if it were a seamless sphere of bluish-green opalescent fluid. This place, dusted lightly with what seemed to be dimly lit stars, enveloped him. He didn't feel so much afloat on it as much as *immersed* or *engulfed in it*. It was beyond immersion...he felt as if he was a part of it, an extension of it. The place had a slight tropical influence which he thought was a bit odd, because this place was devoid of any kind of sound, smell or trade-wind breeze.

He had been here before. His first experience in this eerie surreal place spooked him and he wanted to scream; something... anything to break the silence. But this time it was different; it still had its quirkiness but now it was a familiar place and he enjoyed the 'escape' it was providing.

Jim sat up, reached over the side of the boat and dipped several of his fingers into the mirror-smooth surface, creating tiny cylindrical ripples that radiated outward in slow exaggerated circles as they grew and disappeared into the infinite, deep aqua hue.

Jim smiled because he knew exactly what was about to take place next in this surreal place. He also knew that this was real and wasn't some sort of dream or *déjà vu* type thing. He thought it would be best for him to just lay back and let it play itself out. He intertwined his fingers behind his head and waited for a man named Jonathan to show up, paddling a red canoe. He wondered briefly if the canoe was made of fiberglass or aluminum.

It wasn't long before the red canoe and its' occupant appeared, seemingly out of nowhere, and drifted along side of Jim's little dingy, stopping on cue. Jonathan looked around at the surrounding sky, "Ah, the 'Powers-that-Be' are at it again," he said, nodding his head in acknowledgment. "I never get tired of this place."

Jim's only response was, "Wood."

"Excuse me?"

"I remembered everything about this place, even that you would come paddling up in a red canoe, but I couldn't remember what your canoe was made of. I assumed that it was either fiberglass or aluminum."

"Well, you assumed wrong," Jonathan chuckled. "But it's good that you are choosing to remember things. So why are we here this time?"

"I'm not sure; I just woke up here again," Jim said somewhat baffled.

"Of course you know why, or we wouldn't be here," Jonathan said encouragingly. "We don't have to go through this every time." Jonathan paused, "I do have to say you're starting to remember more quickly how things work, now that it's time. What's the last thing you remember?"

"Well, I remember I was skydiving with Rabina. We were doing a couple of easy formations and I tumbled into her. I think I may have even kicked her in the mouth. Then everything kinda came unglued; we struggled to get stable again…and…and…" Jim's voice trailed off as a chill ran through his body. He finally finished his sentence. "Then we hit the ground. Ah, crap!" he said, looking at Jonathan in disbelief. "I'm dead aren't I?"

"If that's what you want. Remember, it's your choice…"

"Just like that, huh? I get to decide if I want to be alive or dead?"

Jonathan thought for a second and then pursed his lips slightly as he nodded, "Yup, pretty much. It _is_ that simple...and it is always your choice. Deep down in the bowels of your existence, you know that. You also know that life and death walk side by side."

"If I go back, what do I do? Just pick myself up off of the ground, brush myself off and walk away? What do I tell all the people that saw me crash?"

"Your future existence in that world hangs in the balance and you're worried about what to tell the people?" Jonathan asked in disbelief. "Tell them you died...Tell them that you _didn't_ die! Tell them you died but changed your mind and decided to come back... Tell them whatever you want. Tell them all to go to hell if that makes you happy. Oh, I've got an even better idea; just look at them with a devilish grin and say "Oops!", and then just walk away!!. I'd love to see the look on their faces if you did that.

You could tell them anything you want at this point and they will pass it off as babble from a concussion or shock. They'll forgive you for anything you say. They _expect_ you to be delirious; after all you just conked your head after bouncing off the ground at 120 miles an hour. When it's all said and done, you're under no obligation to tell them anything. James; it truly doesn't matter what they think. Don't buy into what THEY are expecting. You are above that now. This life is too short not to be doing what it is you really want to do. That would be your only sin."

Jonathan was silent for a moment and then added, "Maybe you're not ready for what is to come," he said sarcastically. "You know, maybe you should stay dead. That would solve everything for you. After all, that's what _THEY_ are expecting of you; isn't it?" Jonathan paused, letting Jim absorb what had just been said. Then in a more compassionate tone continued. "Jim, be open to all that can be. Choose what it is you want to do in this life, and then just go and do it." Jonathan reached out and touched Jim's arm at the elbow. Jim's whole body tingled as he looked over at Jonathan. "You know you've got things to do. I suggest that you go and do them, but it's your choice,." Jonathan said, his eyes sparkling blue. "We'll talk soon." He nodded at Jim as everything faded to black.

Chapter 2
The Quarry

When Jim opened his eyes again he found himself lying face down on the ground. If it wasn't for the full-face helmet he was wearing, his face would have been buried firmly into the grass and dirt. His body was heavy and sluggish as he rolled over onto his back. A woman knelt beside him, with a dozen or more people huddled behind her staring in amazement.

His mind was foggy and his thoughts disjointed but he was still coherent enough to notice that this woman kneeling beside him was beautiful. Lightly freckled with strawberry blonde hair, her face was familiar but at the moment he couldn't put a name to the face. He thought it was odd how some things were crystal clear while others remained only peripheral…but her face; her face he recognized from somewhere. He knew these were strange observations and under different circumstances he probably would have asked her if she'd like to grab a cup of coffee somewhere. He unstrapped his helmet as she helped him gently pull it from his head. Just as he made an attempt to sit up, she leaned over and kissed him softly on his forehead.

He didn't get a chance for it to really register, as anxious voices interrupted the moment and his mind still raced through a cloud of confusion. He tried to make sense of what was going on as he once again struggled to sit up on his own. The frantic crowd shouted for him to lie still and not to move while others began bombarding him with questions. All of the voices demanded to be heard at the same time, making it all just jumbled white noise in Jim's head. He ran his hands over his face, thinking somehow it

10

was going to erase the chaos around him. What was all the commotion about? In a brilliant flash of clarity, he remembered exactly what brought him to this point in time.

He and one of his friends, Rabina, had collided in mid-air while sky diving, and everything had gone black. Jim knew he had caused the accident. He had been spending all of his time at the drop-zone recently piloting the plane and had neglected his sky diving skills. When Rabina asked him to make the jump with her, his instincts told him he was rusty and he told her of his apprehension, but she mentioned something about it being like riding a bicycle and convinced him that everything would be fine. Normally, a simple coaxing wouldn't have been enough to get Jim to jump, but Rabina was a special friend. She was one of the few people that Jim trusted and had allowed to get close to him. He enjoyed her honesty and laid-back Californian quirkiness. It was her free thinking that had helped influence how he viewed life, and he trusted her completely. Now he regretted letting himself be talked into making the jump. Now it was too late.

He released his parachute harness and rolled to his knees. He then tried to stand up on shaky legs. He did so to a chorus of objections and gasps from the small crowd. "Please, give me some space...I need some space," Jim said as he stood and tried to see past them. "Where's Rabina?" he asked softly. The crowd went mute, not knowing what to say. Jim looked around at the bewildered faces. "What?" he asked. His voice began to tremble, "Where's Rabina? It's not that tough of a question. Where is she? I need to talk to her. I need to apologize!"

A faceless voice from the crowd finally broke the silence and said, "Uh... Jim, how do I say it? She didn't make it. You both hit the ground so hard that you bounced about six feet back into the air and then dropped again like...like... well, kinda like rag-dolls...it was horrible. It doesn't seem real. We thought for sure you were *both* dead. I don't know how you survived. It's a miracle! Are you OK? Of course you're not...you can't be...you've got to be hurt. You should lie back down until the ambulance gets here."

"She can't be dead," Jim said, not knowing if he had actually verbalized it or just thought it to himself. "Where is she? Show me where she is," Jim demanded in a passive panic. The assembly of people once again stood in frozen silence. Jim pleaded, "Don't just

11

stand there; show me where she is!" He looked around in desperation, and then pressed his way through the throng of people. As he staggered forward, the crowd parted, revealing a crumpled body in a black jumpsuit fifty feet in front of him. It was Rabina, her unopened parachute still strapped securely on her back. Jim stumbled through the people on wobbly legs, barely able to stay on his feet. He reached the lifeless body and fell to his knees in tears. "No, no, no…it can't be. It doesn't have to be this way," he whispered to himself, but it was as if he were talking to someone else. The crowd once again enveloped him. A voice from behind him shouted, "An ambulance is on its way. There's nothing you can do for her Jim; she's dead." The voice was familiar; it was Dana, another skydiver, but Jim didn't react to her words.

Jim, still on his knees, sat back and rested his body against his heels. He raised his arms over his head with outstretched hands, gesturing everyone to be quiet. The crowd instantly disappeared from his mind, as if he had mentally pushed them back a hundred yards and out of his consciousness. He was now alone with his lifeless friend in total silence.

He closed his eyes and recalled the conversation he had just had with Jonathan moments ago in the abyss before he had regained consciousness. Jim wiped the tears from his face and with a knowing smile, he leaned over Rabina's limp body and whispered into the ear hole of her helmet. He bowed his head for a few seconds and then stood up on strong confident legs. Completely exhausted but with conviction, Jim extended his hand out to Rabina, expecting her to reach for it. It took several more seconds but her body moved and she slowly lifted her hand toward his. He helped her up into a sitting position and knelt on one knee beside her, resting his hand on her shoulder. He smiled as he looked into her eyes and said, "That was one helluva ride wasn't it?" With glazed eyes, she smiled back but didn't answer.

Jim snapped back from his private world with Rabina and was once again conscious of the crowd buzzing with a mix of confusion and awe. The crowd had grown and pushed closer. Rabina's movement caused gasps and whispers. The whispers gained momentum, becoming a murmur. An uneasy muffled commotion began to circulate through the crowd like a giant tidal wave, building out of control, escalating to a near hysterical frenzy. The horde of people pressed closer, enveloping the two, pushing and tugging at them as if they were rag dolls. The inquisitive crowd continued to press so close that it made it nearly impossible to breathe. The easygoing people that Jim and Rabina had spent most of their free time skydiving with were now become an unruly mob.

The crowd's change in temperament frightened Jim. His gut instinct was to leave immediately and take Rabina with him for her own safety... his *fight or flight* response was screaming at him. He chose 'flight.'

He looked at Rabina and said, "Let's get the hell out of here...NOW!" She nodded in agreement, overwhelmed by all the commotion. Jim wasn't even sure if she understood what he had just said or if she was just agreeing to anything at that point, but at the moment it didn't matter. If she couldn't walk on her own he would have to carry her. He unhooked her harness, letting the dead weight of the parachute fall to the ground behind her. He stood up and once again extended his hand to her. She instinctively grabbed it. He yanked her up to her feet with pure adrenaline and wrapped her arm over his shoulder and his arm around her waist to support her in an attempt to speed their departure. Jim clung tightly to Rabina, shielding her from the crowd, and he wasn't about to let go.

Jim pushed through the crowd with Rabina in tow, their hands clenched tightly together. They made their way to his truck parked near the hanger as the swarm of people followed. Jim was fighting off shock and panic as they got into the truck and locked the doors. His hand shook as he struggled to slide the key into the ignition. He started the truck and pulled away, leaving the drop zone and the mob behind them in a cloud of light gray dust. As they traveled down the gravel road, Jim kept checking the rear view mirror to see if anyone was following them. Surprisingly, no one was.

Neither Jim nor Rabina spoke a word as he drove. The silence continued until Jim was sure they hadn't been followed, and only then did he dare to think about stopping somewhere. He glanced in the rear view mirror one last time before turning onto a narrow rutted path that led to an abandoned stone quarry. Jim was counting on the fact that very few people remembered this place and even fewer came down there. This was where he and his friends came to swim and drink beer when they were in high school, which seemed like a lifetime ago. Jim pulled the truck behind a mound of dirt, out of sight from anyone that might pass by on the road. He parked near the edge of the water-filled quarry; the two got out of the truck and walked over to a huge flat stone by the edge of the water. They climbed up onto the rock and sat in silence for several minutes, quietly regaining their composure.

Jim broke the awkward silence saying, "I had forgotten about this place. I hope everyone else has too."

Rabina, staring out over the water, finally spoke. "Jim, what just happened back there?"

"What do you remember?" he asked.

"Well, the last thing I really remember is leaving the airplane, and I don't remember much after that," she said, bobbing her head slowly in an effort to force more information out of her mouth. "I do remember that we got out of the plane okay, and I remember looking at my altimeter. We were at about eight thousand feet, weren't we?" she asked rhetorically. "I remember grabbing your hands, and then things get fuzzy." She paused again, trying to remember more. "Then everything went dark and it got so...so quiet. The next thing I remember is you blowing in my ear..."

"Just for the record, I didn't blow in your ear; I whispered in it!" Jim shot back with a grin.

"Yeah, I know...I heard you say something."

Jim smiled. "If you hadn't tried to play hero and save my ass from tumbling out of control, we wouldn't have collided and banged our heads. I would have been the only one who had to bounce on the ground."

Rabina's head snapped toward Jim. "Are you saying we're dead? I don't feel dead. We can't be...I don't remember seeing a bright light or a tunnel or any family members who have passed on waiting to greet me. It was just dark."

"No...we're not dead, but we were...well, probably for a little while anyway," he replied somewhat whimsically. He was quiet for a moment and then asked, "Do you remember anything else?"

Rabina stared blankly at Jim for a moment and then responded. "Were we really dead?"

14

"Yeaaah," he said, dragging it out to the point of sounding lighthearted. "We were, but just for a few minutes. Then he repeated his question. "Do you remember anything else?"

"I'm not sure...wait...nah...never mind," she said.

"What?" Jim coaxed.

"Well, it's weird...I do remember being in a dark place with all these tiny white dots off in the distance. It wasn't that bright light, tunnel full of dead loved ones thing that you hear people describe when they've had a near-death experience. It was just a bunch of little penlight-type lights. Kinda disappointing when you stop to think about it," she said. Then she asked excitedly, "Why, what do you remember? Something happened to you, didn't it?"

"Maybe...but I'm not sure if I can explain it." Jim hesitated and then asked, "Do you remember floating?"

"I don't really remember...maybe," she said, shrugging her shoulders. "I might have been...why? Were you floating? You must have been floating. You wouldn't have asked if I was floating if you hadn't been. What do you remember? Tell me, tell me, *tell* me!" Rabina said, like a child wanting to know a secret.

"Okay, okay! Stop talking and I'll tell you what I remember, but you're going to think I'm crazy."

"I hate to be the one to break the news to you, but I've known you were crazy for a long time already, so start talking mister!"

"You're pretty funny for a woman who hit the ground at a hundred and twenty miles an hour."

"Yeah, I know. I guess this whole 'hitting the ground' thing hasn't sunk in yet. None of this has sunk in yet. It's so surreal that it just doesn't make sense. I mean, look, I don't have a bruise on my body except for this fat lip and nothing seems to hurt. That's just not normal."

"Sorry about that fat lip of yours, Rabina. I'm pretty sure I'm responsible for it. I think I may have hit you in the mouth when I did my little tumbling act. I've always said that you should wear a full-face helmet."

"Thank you very much, but I'm not worried about that right now.... Tell me again that you're sure we're not dead?"

"I'm sure."

"Positive?"

"Positive!"

"And you know this how?" Rabina asked.

"I just do."

"Oh, well that helps a lot," she said, unconvinced. She then asked, "Don't you think all this is weird?"

"Well, yeah, but you know… it's all crazy. So many strange things have been happening to me in the last couple of months that it's all kinda dreamlike. I'm not sure what the definition of weird or crazy is anymore. Not long ago I would have thought this was really crazy impossible, you know, but now…not so much."

"Well, I tell you what…I'll shut up for a while and quit askin' questions and you just start talking."

"But it all sounds so strange and bizarre. I'm embarrassed to even tell you."

"Like I said, I already know that you're not right…so just start talking. Seriously, talk!"

"I'm not sure where to begin. This is going to be so hard to explain without going back and telling you everything that has happened since spring."

"Well then, start there."

"You're going to think it's all so weird."

"You already said that, so start….oh yeah, I was going to be quiet. See? I'm being quiet! Look, I'm not saying a word, Rabina said with a smile, trying to prompt him to continue. "And I'll only interrupt you if I have a really good question, okay?

"Okay, okay, now shut up already," he said, returning her smile. "Are you sure that you're ready?"

Rabina nodded.

"Ok, here I go… I was floating in that twilight and I knew I'd been there before."

"When was that?" Rabina inquired.

Jim looked at Rabina with a grin, "You just can't help yourself, can you?"

"What?" she asked innocently.

"I got one sentence out and you had to talk."

"Well, I need to know how you knew you were there before, don't I?"

"Good point, I suppose, but I'll get to that in a little bit. Anyway, everything around me was a deep aquamarine color with those same dim lights you saw. The first time I saw them I thought they were stars."

"Yeah, I remember the color now…that was so cool. Weird, though; I always thought 'dead' would be pitch black with that whole tunnel thing happening," Rabina said, using several exaggerated hand gestures to aid in making her point.

Jim continued on despite Rabina's interruption. "I was in that little inflatable boat again."

"What do you mean, *again*?" Saying that, Rabina's eyes got big and she covered her mouth with her hand, "Oops, I did it again; sorry!" She motioned, encouraging him to continue. "Go on."

"I'm trying to explain as best as I can, but it's just that there are so many parts and pieces to the story. It's hard to condense it all and still have it make sense." Jim thought for a few seconds and then grinned.

"What?" Rabina asked, as if she had done something funny that she wasn't aware of.

"I can do better than tell you about it…I can show you."

Rabina looked at Jim with apprehension. "You can show me what?"

"Trust me," he said and turned to face her directly. "Here, hold my hands and close your eyes." She obeyed as he continued, "Now, take a deep breath and relax."

She nodded and closed her eyes, wiggling her body into a comfortable position. She began to take a deep breath but paused halfway and opened one eye. She looked over at Jim and said, "Wait! Just one thing before we do this."

"What's that?" he asked.

With one eye still closed, she asked, "Are you *sure* that we're not dead?"

"Yes, I'm positive," he said with a crooked grin. "Now close your eyes…excuse me; close your *eye* and take a long, relaxing breath and enjoy this already, damn it!"

Rabina took a deep breath in through her nose, held it for several seconds and then exhaled slowly through her mouth. Jim looked at her and asked, "Are you ready?" She nodded.

Jim closed his eyes and met Rabina in the aquamarine abyss. Together they watched the events that transpired earlier between Jim and Jonathan play out in front of them. It was as if they were actually there next to the boats as it happened, but invisible to the two men engaged in this vision. Jim looked at Rabina and whispered,"I can understand why actors don't like to watch themselves on screen." Rabina remained silent. He then leaned toward her and asked, "I don't sound anything like that, do I?"

Rabina gave Jim a strange look…something between 'you gotta be kidding' and 'quiet, I'm watching this,' but managed to say, "We don't have to whisper. I'm pretty sure they can't hear us… I mean, you can't hear us and no, you don't look ten pounds heavier either." He realized this was a rerun for him but it was an all-new experience for Rabina and she wanted to watch the whole thing, so he remained quiet for the remainder of the *visual transmission*. Once it had played itself to its conclusion, everything went to black and they opened their eyes.

Rabina raised her eyebrows and said, "How cool was that? That was amazing. How'd you do it?"

"I have no clue…" he said with a chuckle. "I'm pretty sure I didn't do anything at all. I just somehow knew it would work."

"So, tell me more about this Jonathan guy in the canoe. How long have you known him? Does he just kinda show up when you need help?"

"Yeah, it does seem that way doesn't it?" Jim answered fondly, and then changed the subject. "Are you hungry? I haven't eaten all day. You probably haven't either."

"Yeah, I could go for something to eat. What are you in the mood for?"

"I'm thinkin' Chinese. How about you?" Jim asked as he stood and offered a hand to Rabina.

"Chinese sounds good," she said with a nod, and smiled at Jim as she reached for his hand. "Wow, this is becoming a habit."

"What's that, feeding you?" Jim asked.

"No, you *never* feed me; I'm talking about extending me a helping hand," she said. She got to her feet on her own and brushed the rock dust from the seat of her pants.

"That's just how it worked out."

"By the way, what did you whisper in my ear at the drop-zone?"

Jim shot her a devilish smile.

"You're not going to tell me are you?" she asked, somewhat surprised. "Are you ever going to tell me?"

"Maybe... in time."

"You didn't say anything, did you? You just blew in my ear...I knew it. You probably stuck your tongue in it too...Yuck," she said kiddingly, taunting him, hoping he would tell her what he had said. "Well, whatever you said...thanks."

"No thanks required...I'm sure you'll return the favor sometime."

"Wow, you say that with such conviction; is there something you're not telling me?"

"No, it's just this gut feeling again, and lately it's been dead on...no pun intended. I think that's why we're all here."

"Explain, please."

"I think we're all here to help one another. It's as if we each are a note in the song and need to come together with others to create the grand symphony. At least that's what seems to be happening."

"That's a great analogy. How do you get everyone to share that idea?"

Jim shrugged his shoulders and said, "I guess I add that to the list of questions that need answers."

Jim and Rabina climbed back into the truck and prepared to head into town.

19

Chapter 3
The Door

Rabina's passenger door wasn't even completely closed when she said, "So, tell me more about this guy, Jonathan. You were so vague before."

"I was vague only because he is such an enigma. Once again, where do I begin?" Jim said, talking more to himself than to her.

"Well, how did you meet him? Where did he come from? Is this guy like, a real person?"

"Those are all great questions and I will answer them as best I can... Okay, I think he's real... I met him at the drop-zone this past spring and ever since then he just shows up." Jim stopped talking as he backed the truck up and turned around. He pulled out of the quarry, looking briefly in the direction of the drop-zone and then turned the opposite way...toward the real world of traffic, people and food. Rabina noticed Jim seemed wrapped in his own little world; probably mulling over her last questions. She didn't want to interrupt his thinking just yet. She let the silence continue for a moment and then leaned over and turned on the radio. They were both quietly content, lost in their own thoughts with the classic rock station playing in the background.

The mood was broken when the news came on, as it did at the top of every hour. The voice on the radio led off with a brief account of the accident at the drop-zone involving them earlier that day. *"Two people were involved in a skydiving incident near Pulaski earlier today. Details are sketchy at this time, but it is believed Jim Riggs and Rabina Lynn's parachutes failed to open after they collided while skydiving. The two sustained*

undetermined injuries and sought medical treatment on their own."
The voice wrapped up the two-minute segment with sports and local weather, followed by a commercial.

Rabina looked at Jim and said, "Wow, that was pretty freaky to hear, wasn't it?"

"Yeah, it was."

"Do you think we'll run into anyone we know at the Chinese place? I'm not ready to try explaining to someone what happened today. To be honest, I'm not sure I can even explain it to myself yet. What could we possibly say? *"Hi, how are you? Yeah, we fell from eight thousand feet and hit the ground so hard that we're told we bounced about six feet back into the air. We both died, but then we got up and walked away without a scratch or bruise. We're OK now, the Rangoon are delicious, see you later, have a nice day!"* Rabina shook her head. "I can't do it," she added.

"Yeah, you're probably right," Jim said. "What do you say instead of doing Chinese, we stop at that little grocery store on County S and pick up a couple hunks of animal flesh and a bottle of wine and grill out at my place? It will be easier to talk there, and we won't have to worry about running into anyone."

"Yeah, that sounds like a better choice right now...do you have a corkscrew at your house? Better yet, can we buy the 'good' wine with the twist off cap?" Rabina asked, intentionally trying to lighten the mood.

"Hey, even good wines are coming with screw caps now, but maybe if you're good, I'll buy you a whole carafe in a cardboard box," Jim added with a grin.

"Hey, don't knock it; I've got a carton of that on top of my refrigerator."

"Whatever floats your boat," Jim said, and then added, "You know, my old flight instructor, Josie, gave me a bottle of wine she made herself. I've been saving it for some special occasion. I think this qualifies."

"Is it any good?"

"Very."

"Well, why don't you save it for another time? I think I'm in the mood for quantity tonight, not quality, so we better get the cheap stuff... and lots of it!"

They stopped at the 'mom and pop' store that sold a little bit of everything, from clothes pins to freshly butchered beef and pork. They wandered through its narrow aisles of neatly packed shelves, picked up what they needed for their impromptu meal, including a *box* of wine, and continued on their way to Jim's place.

His house was nestled in the woods, far enough off of the road that most people didn't even know there was a home at the end of the long winding driveway. He'd been asked by people on occasion why he had built the house where people couldn't see it. His standard answer was, "You just answered your own question." That response usually left the questioner more confused than ever.

They parked in the left stall of his oversized three-car garage cluttered with expensive toys. The stall was closest to the house entry. Jim grabbed the bag containing the groceries and Rabina pulled the box of wine from the passenger floor and they headed inside. As they walked to the door, Rabina looked at the array of vehicles around her. There was a long boat with a huge shiny engine poking out the top, several motorcycles and a couple of four-wheelers. He even had a car lift with one car parked above another just to make room for everything. "Boy, I've never been inside your garage before. I didn't realize that you had so many nice toys!"

"Thanks," Jim said. "This is what happens when you don't have kids to throw money at. I've come to realize all these *things* don't make you any happier, but of course I found this out AFTER I bought them all," he said with a chuckle. He opened the door and led her to the kitchen. "Do you mind tearing open that box of wine while I fire up the grill?" he asked.

"That sounds like a plan," she replied. "I like how you think...you do the work and I get to drink wine and watch. I'm ready to put a dent in this box of wine and I have got just the glass to do it with." She retrieved a larger tumbler from the open shelf near the sink.

"Well, we certainly have plenty of it," Jim said. He looked over at his desk and saw the message light blinking on his answering machine. He walked over and checked it. "Twenty-three messages?! I've never had this many messages...not even when I was gone on vacation for two weeks. I'm not in the mood to listen to them now. I'll do that later....maybe tomorrow," he said as he walked away from the desk.

Once the wine was poured and the steaks were sizzling on the grill, they settled into the cedar lounge chairs on his deck. This was the first chance they really had had to seriously relax after all the commotion of the day.

Rabina looked over at Jim. "Did today really happen? I mean, really...did those things happen to us? It's like I know it happened, but it just seems way too weird. You know what I mean?"

"I know exactly what you mean, but they did really happen. I was in the same disbelief when things started happening to me a couple of months ago too, but I'm kinda getting used to it."

"You've gotten used to things like dying? Does that really seem *normal* to you?" Rabina shot at him.

"Well... no, I won't go that far; that was a first for me too," he said with a slight chuckle. "But I have had some very strange things happen to me."

"Jim, this just doesn't feel right. Something's not right, I feel as if I shouldn't be here..."

"I felt that same way after I went skydiving with Jonathan."

"You're comparing how you felt skydiving with my feelings that I should be dead?" she snapped.

"Rabina, relax! Take a big drink of your pseudo-wine and let me explain before you get all bent out of shape here. I'll tell you what I'm talkin' about in a minute, but you gotta believe me, it's not that scary. I've been learning that we're not supposed to *be* anything...we just *are*."

"That's so Zen of you," Rabina said sharply.

"Hey, don't jump on my ass...I'm just telling you what I've been learning," Jim said, defending himself.

"Sorry, I'm getting these edgy sensations. I think it's finally sinking in that I did just fall to my death from an airplane... you know?" She began to laugh.

"What?" Jim asked, wondering why she was laughing.

"Did you hear what I just said? Did I just say I fell out of an airplane to my death? It just sounds so funny it can't be real. I'm going to wake up pretty soon and call you to tell you about this vivid dream I had..." She paused. "But I know it really did happen. I've got the fat lip to prove it."

"I said I was sorry," Jim said with a smile. "Now drink that wine; hopefully it will numb the pain....and mellow you out a little bit."

"Good idea! More wine, give me more wine," she mockingly demanded! "And then, tell me more about your *Adventures with Jonathan*. Hey, that would be a great title for a book, don't you think?"

Jim filled her glass about half way and began to pour some for himself when Rabina said, "You know, I'm told that an optimist sees my glass as half full, so that must make me a pessimist because I see it as *half empty*! What are you saving it for? It's not going to evaporate...fill it up, already!"

"Sure thing. You may see the glass half empty, but if you were an engineer you'd see the glass as twice as big as it needs to be," Jim said as he filled her tumbler glass almost to the brim.

"Well, good thing I'm not an engineer 'cause I picked this particular glass for a reason, and I see it as just the right size. So now...tell me more about this Jonathan guy and why dropping to your death doesn't seem to weird you out."

"The first time I saw Jonathan was this past spring at the drop zone. There were a lot of students that particular day and for some reason I was the only pilot. I don't remember why I was the only pilot around, but anyway, by noon I had already flown five or six loads of students. I decided to take a break because my butt was getting sore from being in that hard plane seat all morning, and I was probably a little bored as well. I taxied over and parked the plane by the fuel tanks and then milled around for awhile. I listened in on little bits and pieces of conversations but I was hungry so I thought I'd eat my lunch and take a little break over at the picnic table."

Rabina interrupted, "Get to the good stuff already!"

24

"Okay, okay…there were two people who caught my attention that day. The first was a woman in her mid-thirties and…" Jim stopped suddenly in mid-sentence. His eyes widened in an expression of astonishment. "Oh, my god!" he exclaimed.

"What?" Rabina asked, "What is it?"

"Ohmygod, ohmygod, Oh…My…God!" he said, as if unable to say anything else.

"What…tell me. Come on, what is it? What's wrong? What?"

"It was *her*!" he finally said.

"Her, who?"

"The strawberry blonde! The woman who was kneeling beside me when I regained consciousness today…oh my god; I can't believe it. It's the same woman. And I just remembered… she gave me a little peck on the forehead as I tried to get up today. Wow, she kissed me," Jim said in amazement.

"Back up, lover boy. She's the same woman - what?" Rabina was confused.

"The woman who was kneeling by me today is the same woman I was so infatuated with that day back in spring."

"And?"

"And that is just so weird."

"You were just saying that nothing seems weird to you anymore. Now you're saying it's weird."

"Well, I stand corrected."

"Jim, maybe she just happened to be at the drop zone. What's so odd about seeing her again today?"

"But that's what's so weird…I never saw her any time in between, but there she was today!"

"Probably just a coincidence, or maybe she's been there and you just didn't notice her."

"Oh no, if she had been there, trust me, I would have noticed. I looked for her every weekend."

"Well then, maybe she's a doctor, or nurse or something and came over to help. Tell me more about how you met her."

"Well, I didn't actually meet her. She just showed up at the drop zone that day, looking marvelous. She was long and lean. I bet she was close to six feet tall in heels."

"What was she doing wearing heels at the drop zone?"

"Well…in her defense, they weren't real high ones. I gotta tell you, they worked for her."

"A little strange, but go on."

"She had these cute little freckles and strawberry blonde hair that ended near her waist with just a bit of wave. She had on a pair of worn jeans that fit so well and this little white sleeveless blouse that was unbuttoned just far enough to reveal a bit of the lacy lavender bra underneath, and it was tied in front with her tanned belly button showing."

Rabina interrupted Jim again, "She was tanned and dressed like that at the drop zone…in spring? It sounds like a bit much."

"No, it really wasn't, not at all, not on *her* anyway. I know it sounds like it was over the top, but like I said, it worked for her. She exuded pheromones," he said with a slight chuckle. "She was classy, not trashy."

"Well, you make it sound as if she should be in a Victoria's Secret ad instead of the drop zone. I hate women who look that good. And tanned besides…they make me look bad," she said with a grin.

"It wasn't like that at all. She didn't stand out because of how she was dressed. She looked good… Again, she looked "classy." She turned heads, especially mine, but there was more than just her beauty…it was as if she were glowing. She had a grace and confidence about her that you don't often see. I swear she radiated an *energy*."

"She didn't strike me as the nurse type, but I'd play doctor with her anytime! She was simply a delight to watch and I couldn't stop staring at her. There was something in her eyes when she looked at me that took me to another place. It was like I knew her from somewhere. Those green eyes of hers were hypnotic."

"Delightful? Glowing? Hypnotic? Please! Now you're scaring me…" Rabina said lightly. "Besides, that's definitely more information than I need to know."

"I can't explain it any other way. We locked eyes for an instant, and she kinda did a double-take as if she recognized me too."

"What did you say to her?"

"Well, that's the thing...I didn't say anything. We just smiled at each other and she eventually turned her attention to the picture board on the wall. She looked back at me one more time to see if I was still watching her...and of course I was."

"Why didn't you go and talk to her?"

"I'm not quite sure...well, yes I do. I was afraid of getting shot down. I'm sure she was at least ten years younger than me." Jim thought for a moment and then added, "No, it was more than that...it was as if I knew it just wasn't the right time. Do you know what I mean?"

"All I can say is...no guts, no glory," Rabina answered

"Yeah, yeah, I know. Anyway, that's the story on her. Do you think it means anything?"

"Time will tell, won't it?"

"I get real tired of hearing that."

"Patience, Jim," Rabina said, patting Jim's folded hands.

"I'm tired of hearing that too. I've been patient. It's time already!"

"It'll happen soon enough," Rabina replied.

Jim nodded, saying, "The other person who piqued my curiosity that day was Jonathan. He was a lanky guy, probably in his early sixties. His skin was dark and leathery with deep character creases in his face and a couple-day stubble. He was balding on top with the remaining salt and pepper hair pulled back into a short braid, and he wore a little gold hoop earring in his left ear. He was wearing a faded yellow button-down shirt with the sleeves rolled up past his elbows and that little pocket in the left corner of the chest and baggy blue jeans that hung loosely from his almost nonexistent hips. He had a tattoo of a feather on his left forearm and wore a pair of beat-up moccasins that had seen better days. Yet for all the wear, they still had some of the red, black and white beads attached. This guy just wouldn't have looked right with real shoes on."

Jim continued, "Jonathan had such a presence about him; different from the blonde woman, but there was something in his body language that told me he wasn't a weekend adventurer. I knew he had done it all when it came to skydiving. Just the way that he carried himself, I knew he was a SKYGOD."

"Wow, you can be very descriptive when you want to be. You described them both very well," Rabina said sincerely.

"I have my moments," Jim said with a quick modest grin and a shrug of his shoulders, but continued so he wouldn't lose his point. "The strange thing was, I felt like I had met him before. Jonathan saw me looking at him and he gave me a wink and a familiar smile as if he knew me too."

"What did you do?" Rabina asked.

"I just nodded back. Anyway, I divided my time watching the woman and Jonathan. I felt like I was watching a Yin/Yang thing going on; beauty versus function, youth versus age... one knowing nothing about skydiving and the other knowing everything. And for obvious reasons, I watched her more than I watched Jonathan. She was very easy to watch as she mingled through the different groups of people, content in observing everything around her. She seemed quiet and reserved. Jonathan, on the other hand, was boisterous. His body gyrated and his arms and hands flailed in every direction as he talked. You could sense his deep conviction in what he was saying, even though he spoke at about 501 words a minute. His black eyes shimmered when he spoke and he never left anyone out of the conversation. He seemed to be energized by the interest of the listeners. Everyone felt as if they were the only one he was talking to. The man definitely had a gift."

"Jim, I'm not trying to be rude, but what does any of this have to do with what happened today?"

"Well, I thought I'd give you all the background and some details because I'm not really sure what might be important. I'd rather give you too much information than not enough. Do you mind?"

"No, but if this is going to take all night, you better fill my glass again," Rabina said with a smile. She held up her empty glass, shaking it between her thumb and index finger. She continued, "Hey, why don't we do that thing we did at the quarry?"

"We can give it a try," Jim said as he filled her glass again. He moved the steaks to the edge of the grill, away from the high heat. They turned their chairs toward each other. Rabina took a drink of her wine and then put her hands in Jim's. They sat in silence for a minute or two but nothing seemed to be happening. Jim was about ready to give up on the idea when an image of him walking over to a picnic bench under an oak tree across the parking lot of the drop zone came into view. "It's working," Jim said quietly to Rabina.

She responded with a "Shhhhhhh."

As the scene unfolded, Jim sat down on the bench and popped the lid off the cooler that contained the meager lunch he had packed on his way out of the door that morning. He had grabbed a baloney sandwich from the refrigerator that had gone uneaten from the weekend before. He though that the mayo may have gone bad but trusted that the baloney would still be good, given the fact that it had the shelf life of plutonium. Next to the sandwich was a lukewarm can of orange soda and a banana so ripe that his mother would have used it to make banana bread days ago.

Propped up against the inside edge of the cooler was a spiral notebook. This was his makeshift journal, damp with condensation. He had scribbled notes to himself for years on scraps of paper, backs of envelopes, anything that was handy when he had an inspiration. A girlfriend finally gave him a little book with blank pages to scribble in and now he was somewhat more organized and kept his notes limited to a couple of notepads and that little book. Jotting down ideas and observations was just something that he did and it made him feel good.

He ate the sandwich, including the bluish-green mold portions of the crust. He drank the warm soda, swirling the can from time to time to get rid of some of the carbonation, but the banana stayed in the cooler... he wasn't that desperate yet.

After he finished eating, he sprawled out on top of the picnic table and propped the cooler lid under his head like a pillow. He decided to close his eyes and soak up some of the warm sunshine before the jumpers needed him back in the airplane.

Red-orange diatom specks floated before his eyes as the warm sunlight penetrated through his eyelids. He entertained himself for a while watching the little things float around under translucent lids. He chuckled at how easily he could be amused. His mind filled with thoughts of what he might pick up for dinner and what might be on TV that night. Then everything began to blur as his body relaxed. He was no longer aware of his arms and legs as he drifted off into la-la land. He was camping on the edge of sleep as the world around him faded into a foggy white mist.

As the mist cleared, he found himself sitting comfortably on a hillside overlooking a quiet emerald green meadow. Prairie grass softly swaying back and forth like rolling ocean waves caught in an invisible surge as the breeze worked its way through the meadow. Deer grazed in the uncut field near the edge of a glistening stream. The view was breathtakingly serene, a perfect landscape.

In this perfect landscape Jim noticed a door standing oddly in the stream a couple hundred feet in front of him. It was an old fashioned paneled door, similar to the ones he remembered being in his grandparents' home. The door had many peeling layers of paint, with its most recent layer being a muted shade of powder blue. It wasn't attached to anything. There was no frame, walls or bracing; nothing to keep it from falling, and yet there it stood. It was an odd sight, but he chose not to concern himself with it. He was enjoying the fact that he didn't have to think too deeply about anything at the moment.

A masculine voice broke the silence. "James." Jim turned slowly to see who had called his name. He took his time, not wanting to lose the *light* feeling he was experiencing.

Standing twenty feet from him was a form, back lit by the sun. Jim could tell by the size and outline was that of a man, but the brilliant sun behind the man obscured his face. Jim raised his hand over his eyes in a futile attempt to block the glare of the sun. He squinted into the glare and said, "Hello?"

"Do you mind if I join you?" the man asked, and waited for an answer.

Jim paused, still not totally coherent, then said, "Ah, sure. I mean no, I don't mind. Have a seat." He awkwardly stood to greet the man. As the man stepped closer, Jim recognized him as the man he had been watching earlier at the drop zone. It was Jonathan.

"Oh. Hi. I saw you over by the hanger before." Jim continued, "You didn't happen to bring that cute strawberry blonde along with you?"

"Yes you did, and sorry, no I didn't," he replied with the same radiating smile that Jim had noticed earlier.

Jim gave him a puzzled look, so Jonathan elaborated. "Yes, you did see me by the hanger. In fact, I'm still there talking to everyone. And no, I didn't bring the strawberry blonde with me. I must say, you've got good taste in women; she is a pretty thing."

"Too bad," was all Jim could think to say. He extended his hand in a welcoming gesture and said, " You look so familiar...it seems as though I know you from somewhere."

"Yes, I'm sure we've met somewhere; it will come to you in time," Jonathan said as he reached out and shook Jim's hand. His grip was firm but not intimidating. He changed the subject, saying, "If I'm interrupting your solitude, I can leave."

"No, no, that's quite alright. There's plenty of view for the both of us." Then Jim added, "I was just wondering about that door down there in the stream. Do you know anything about it?" Jim asked as he pointed in the general direction of the creek. "I don't know why anyone would go through the trouble of putting it there. Do you think it's someone's idea of art?"

"What door?" Jonathan asked casually.

"That door right out there in the..." Jim sentence trailed off to an inaudible mumble as he turned to see the same beautiful emerald landscape, this time minus the old door. "There was a door out there in the stream," Jim said, slightly mystified.

"A door?" Jonathan asked, as if Jim was hallucinating.

"Yes, a door!" Jim said in rebuttal.

"What kind of door was it?"

"An old one; you know, the ones with the inset rectangular panels."

"Like at Grandmas' house?" Jonathan asked.

"EXACTLY!"

"Never saw it."

"Oh..."

There was a short pause in the question and answering and then Jonathan asked, "Did you put it there?"

"What, the door? No, I didn't put it there!"

"Are you sure?"

"Yes, I'm quite sure."

"Was the door open or closed?" Jonathan inquired.

"That's a strange question. How can you tell? Closed, I guess. It was just a door. Why would it matter if it was opened or closed?"

"Your first instinct was right, it was closed," he said, confirming Jim's answer. "If it had been open, you'd have known".

"So, you did see it!"

"Nope."

"Then how would you know it was closed?"

"Just a gut feeling I guess," Jonathan quipped.

"And you don't find it strange that I would see a door in the middle of nowhere, and then it just disappears?"

"Not really. It's your world and you can create it any which way that trips your trigger. Thoughts and doors, as you just suggested, come and go, open and shut. It's kind of a cosmic law," he replied matter-of-factly.

"You mean that figuratively, right?"

Jonathan shrugged his shoulders and said, "If you choose." Then he added, "You've heard the old adage: 'When one door closes, another opens'?"

"Yeah, but I never took that literally."

"Well, most people don't actually *see* the doors as you did. That's a privilege usually reserved for people who carry on conversations with themselves as they search through dumpsters for lunch." Jonathan continued, "That door – well, to be more precise, the manifestation of a door, is a metaphor for you. Don't you see…a door in the middle of a stream? It's a choice that needs to be made!" Jonathan looked at Jim, waiting for some response. Jim just looked back at him without much of an expression, not knowing if Jonathan was telling him the truth or if he was simply entertaining himself with a bizarre explanation.

Jonathan continued, "These choices, or in this case *doors*, open and close each time we make a decision in our lives, while the stream continues to move on its merry way unconcerned by your choice. A lot of these doors are open all the time; they're actually more like a doorway, just waiting for us to waltz on through any time we choose. Then there are those that slam shut if you don't step through when the opportunity presents itself. These doors can only be opened again after we've learned our lesson and are ready to move on. And finally, there are the doors that we occasionally bang our heads on, trying to force them open. Ultimately, you choose which doors are there and which to open."

"What does it mean if the door was closed?" Jim asked.

"It means it wasn't opened, James!" Jonathan said bluntly.

"I know that! Please quit stating the obvious," Jim said in a raised voice.

Jonathan knew exactly what Jim was trying to ask, but for some reason wasn't answering him. "Well, say what you mean. If you ask the question properly, it usually answers itself," he said.

Jim chose his words carefully. "OK, what is the symbolic meaning of the manifestation of the door being closed?"

"You tell me," Jonathan said.

"Ah, come on; that's garbage!" Jim snapped. "You're probably making this all up as you go along."

Jonathan's expression changed instantly, becoming very stoic. "Don't we all?"

"Excuse Me?"

"The truth? In a nut shell; if the door was closed, it meant that you weren't open to learning the lesson that was before you."

Jim wasn't sure why, but he was overcome with an urge to cry. He bit his tongue in an effort to keep the tears from forming as he wiped his nose.

There was an extremely long silence as Jonathan stared at the ground, grinding the toe of his moccasin into the dirt as he searched for words. He raised his head, and as their eyes met, the hair on

33

Jim's neck prickled. With some reservation Jonathan finally said, "James, it's time. It's time once again."

"It's time again for what?" Jim asked.

"Jim, it's time, wake up, its time." Jim opened his eyes to see Dana, one of the jump masters, standing next to him. Jim realized that he was still on the picnic table. He looked toward the hanger and found Jonathan still entertaining a small crowd with animated conversation.

Dana looked at Jim and asked, "Are you okay? Boy, you were sound asleep! I hated to wake you up, but we better finish with these students if we want to get to Mark's wedding later."

"Yeah, I'll be right there," Jim said as he sat up. He reached into the cooler, pulled out his notebook and scribbled.

1) Door in stream

2) Skygod

3) Doorways/Choices/Lessons

Jim slid the notebook back into the cooler and started back to the crowd when he remembered something else. Not wanting to forget the last fleeting impression of his encounter with Jonathan, he reached back into the cooler and made one more entry:

4) Sometimes, what's important is the question!

Just as before, the entire scene faded to black...

Chapter 4
The Wedding

Jim and Rabina found themselves once again facing each other as they had been, still on Jim's deck.

Rabina was the first to speak. "Wow…that was great! Why didn't you tell me about all this when it happened?"

"Are you ready to tell the world about what happened to you today?" Jim asked, knowing that was the shortest way of answering her question.

"Ah, I see what you mean. It's really hard to believe any of this even when it's happened to you, isn't it?" Rabina replied.

"Hence…the reason why we are hiding out here in my backyard tonight instead of being served Chinese food from column B! If I would have mentioned any of this before today, you would have thought I was nuts. Besides, I wasn't sure if it actually happened or if I was having some sort of psychotic episode."

"Psychotic episode? That was so cool, how could you think that it was caused by mental illness?"

"You don't understand; I couldn't tell if any of it was real, plus that was just the start of everything weird. It seemed as if the level of weirdness had escalated exponentially since then, right up to what happened to us today."

"Why, what else has happened to you?"

"Remember earlier when I made the comparison between you being alive right now, with my skydiving with Jonathan, and you jumped all over my ass for it?"

"Yeah…sorry…just frayed nerves, I guess. What about it?"

"It's just more of that weird stuff."

"I'd like to hear it all!"

"I don't know…it's really out there…"

"Let's see…so far today, I've fallen to my death and walked away… without a scratch no less; then watched two of your life altering experiences first hand. So yeah, I think I'm ready."

"When you put it that way…yeah, I guess you are ready, aren't you?" Jim said with a grin.

"But I think I'll have a little more wine just to be on the safe side." Rabina raised her glass, drinking the remainder of her wine and then looked at Jim saying, "Ah…okay, now I'm ready."

"Do you want my version of what happened, or do you want to see if we can make that whole '*experience thing*' work again?"

"Well Jim, you do tell a pretty good story, but the '*experience thing*' is so cool because it puts me right there with you as it happened. It gives me the sights and sounds, even the smells of the place. And to be perfectly honest, you do get a bit long-winded about certain things. You should have been a preacher or a politician."

"But I thought you liked my stories."

"I do, but I'm a woman and I really don't want to hear about a skinny strawberry blonde *babe*."

"But she really is a 'babe,' and she wasn't skinny…she was just-right slender," Jim said with a huge grin.

"Just bring on the next installment of your experience, lover-boy," she said with an even bigger, full-tooth smile as she extended her hands in front of her in an attempt to get things started.

Once again they held each others' hands hoping to bring on the vision. This time, as the two relaxed into the calm, Jim opened his eyes and saw a faint blue iridescent glow surrounding Rabina's body that extended across to him and up his arms, as far as he could see. Jim wondered if the blue glow had enveloped his entire body as it had Rabina's. He soon forgot about it as the new scene came into focus.

This new installment was a continuation of the previous one. It began with Jim at the controls of a DeHavilland Beaver, the group's jump plane. The 'beaver' had a nine-cylinder engine, producing four-hundred and fifty horse-power and a mellow growl as it flew. The six passengers sat behind Jim, all dressed in jumpsuits, helmets, goggles and parachutes, ready to exit the plane when they achieved the right altitude.

As the plane climbed, they passed the time engaged in their own thoughts or communicated with basic sign language due to the overwhelming noise of the engine. Jim leaned over to Dana, one of the jump masters, and tapped his index finger to his wrist as if asking what time it was.

Dana lifted his right arm and shook the watch on his wrist free from inside his jumpsuit sleeve and yelled over the engine noise. "It's twenty to three; why?"

Jim yelled back, "I was just thinking, you know Mark and Lisa invited all of us to their wedding, right?"

"Yeah, we figured we'd all go to the reception together about 6 o'clock. What about it?"

"The ceremony at the church was at two o'clock and I'm guessing that it should be getting over right about now."

Dana looked at Jim with a blank expression on his face, not getting Jim's point.

"What do you say, we drop in on the wedding a little early?" Jim said with a devilish grin.

Dana looked puzzled at first and then his eyes lit up as Jim's idea finally sunk in. "Gee, do you think we should?" Dana replied cynically with a grin from ear to ear.

Jim dropped the nose of the plane, pulled it into a left bank and leveled off as they now were headed for the center of town. The plane was soon circling high over the church's steeple.

The timing was near perfect, as the wedding party was just beginning to exit the church. Jim throttled the massive engine back to an idle and slowed the aircraft enough for the jumpers to exit. He glanced at the airspeed indicator and then yelled, "Jump run boys and girls; make it a good one. Say "hi" to Mark and Lisa for me and tell them that I expect some of those ham and wedding roll sandwiches, okay? Oh, and some cake too!"

One after another, the jumpers disappeared out of the door as if being sucked out of the plane by a giant vacuum. Jim banked left, watching the jumpers free-fall for a thousand feet and then deploy their chutes to posture themselves for the impromptu visit. The jumpers all landed on the strip of lawn between the church building and the cemetery.

Once the jumpers were safely on the ground and a crowd had encircled them, Jim felt a bit left out and decided it was his turn to congratulate the newly married couple. Pushing the yoke forward as he kicked left rudder and opposite aileron, performing a slip into a shallow dive as if he were on a strafing run. He flew just over the tops of a row of oak trees spaced 50 feet apart along the side of the church, as he rocked the wings back and forth. He made a second pass over the church as the jumpers, carrying their chutes against their chests like bundles of dirty laundry, crowded into limousines along with the wedding party. It was an odd sight and Jim hoped someone was recording all of it. Mark and Lisa wouldn't forget this day for a long time!

Jim turned back south to the airport, found the grass runway at the drop zone and landed. He taxied alongside the hanger and was barely out of the cockpit when a caravan of honking limousines came rolling down the gravel road with a plume of dust trailing behind them. The limos hadn't come to a complete stop when the doors swung open in unison and he instantly heard giggles and chatter. The cloud of dust that had trailed them rolled in and engulfed the limousines as the jumpers stepped out of the cars carrying their bundles of colorful nylon, followed immediately by the wedding party. Mark appeared with his bride Lisa as the cloud of dust began to settle. When Mark saw Jim, he parted from his new wife and the rest of the crowd and walked directly toward him. He was carrying the distinctive blue bottle of Cabo Wabo Reposado tequila, a 110-proof tequila produced by the rock star Sammy Hagar in his hand.

"Where are the sandwiches and cake I ordered? I'm a very hungry pilot," Jim said, knowing that he hadn't really been forgotten in all of the festivities.

"I can't help you there," Mark answered. "You'll have to come to the reception tonight if you want to be fed, but maybe something like this will quench your thirst for now." He raised the bottle of Cabo. "And thanks a lot for dropping in on us like you did; nice touch…very thoughtful. Dana said the whole thing was your idea. That's something that will keep people talking!" Mark added, "We recorded the whole thing, even your fly-by at tree top level. You better be nice to me or I'll send a copy of it to the FAA! You certainly made things exciting for the guests. Thanks again."

"It was our pleasure. Congratulations. Now since you didn't bring me any food, at least quit teasing me and give me that bottle you've been waving in my face since you got here; I could use a drink!"

Jim grabbed the bottle of tequila, only to find it empty. He looked at Mark with an exaggerated lower lip as if he were a pouting three year old. "Don't cry good buddy; step this way," Mark said, motioning Jim to follow him. They walked around to the back of the limo and opened the trunk lid, exposing a variety of beers and several bottles of booze packed on ice in the biggest cooler Jim had ever seen.

Mark retrieved two fresh bottles of the smooth Cabo tequila and handed them both to Jim. "Here are Juan and Jose; they're a set of twins for you, one for each hand. They will put a smile back on your face, and probably put you into a coma if you drink them both. Take good care of them, they're orphans. But right now, I better get back to my wife before she's my EX-wife!" With that, Mark patted Jim on the back and moved back toward the buzzing crowd.

The day was coming to an end, with only a glimmer of red and orange still hanging in the sky as the sun slid below the horizon. Jim felt good because he and the jumpers had added to the wedding experience. He smiled at the fact that he now had a bottle of good tequila in each hand.

The wedding party regrouped in the waning light and drove off for the reception hall. The combination of a hectic day and the abrupt silence with the departure of the overly excited people left Jim with a welcomed calm. He wondered where that strawberry blonde might be.

The horizon was now a fiery red stripe that soon would be extinguished. He knew he had to make a decision to go to the reception, go home, or start a fire and settle in right there at the hanger with the Cabo twins.

Jim wasn't in the mood for the high-spirited crowd at the reception hall, but he wasn't ready to go home either. He chose to start a fire, drink tequila and see what the evening brought him. Maybe he'd even spend the night in the hanger, which he did from time to time. He started a fire in the pit by the picnic table across the parking lot from the hanger and picked up one of the orphaned bottles Mark had graciously donated earlier. He cracked the seal, removed the cap and tossed it over his shoulder into the darkness behind him. He sat quietly, sipping tequila straight from the bottle and staring into the fire, watching as it eventually settled into a dim glow of embers. Having used up all of the available wood without destroying the chair he was sitting in, Jim decided to move his party-of-one to the hanger, slide into a sleeping bag on the couch, find a movie and watch it until he nodded off to sleep. He wished he had a bag of popcorn.

Chapter 5
The Jump

Jim was just about to make his move toward the hanger when he saw headlights bouncing through the darkness. The vehicle made its way down the country road leading to the drop zone. A small, faded blue pick-up truck pulled under the yard light in the parking lot, turned around and slowly backed up, stopping ten feet from the fire pit. The brake lights flashed off along with the sound from its decayed exhaust system, leaving the unmistakable music of Pink Floyd's *Dark Side of the Moon* resonating from within the darkened cab. The cerebral music went silent as the dome light flickered on and the driver door squeaked open... and then once again, all was silent.

Sliding out of the seat was a familiar form. It wasn't the tall strawberry blonde. The silhouette and mannerisms were definitely masculine. As the man stepped closer, the light of the fire confirmed that it was indeed Jonathan.

"No, I'm not that attractive blonde of the female persuasion you were hoping for, but I thought you could use some firewood," he said as if he was reading Jim's mind. He then continued, "This should take the chill out of the air." He dropped the tailgate, revealing several rows of neatly stacked firewood. Jim didn't know how Jonathan knew he was out of wood, but he wasn't going to look a gift horse in the mouth.

Jim looked at Jonathan, saying nothing at first. What could he say? Jim hadn't actually met the man, and had only seen this guy in a crowd. After all, having dreamed about him earlier in the day didn't count as actually *'meeting him'*. Now, here he was - Jonathan, delivering a stack of wood just when he needed it...sweet! These thoughts ran through Jim's tequila-impaired mind. He wasn't sure if Jonathan was even his real name. Jim decided to wait for a better time to talk as he grabbed the bottle of booze cradled between his feet and raised it toward Jonathan with an outstretched arm.

At the sight of the gesture, Jonathan disappeared, head and shoulders, back through the opened window of the truck cab and reappeared with a plastic cup he apparently retrieved from somewhere on the seat or dashboard. He walked over and sat down on a lawn chair next to Jim. He inspected the inside of the cup by firelight, wiped something from the bottom with his finger and then turned it upside down, tapping out whatever it was that he had dislodged. Jonathan took the bottle from Jim's hand and nodded with appreciation. "Wow, this is the really good stuff." He poured himself about three fingers of the booze into the cup, and then raised the cup in Jim's direction as if he was making a toast.

Jonathan looked around and asked, "Are you sure I'm not intruding?"

Jim thought it odd because that's what Jonathan had said to him in the dream. Jim figured this gave him the perfect segue to mention the dream. "It's funny you should say that," he said. "While I was catching a little nap this afternoon on the picnic table I had a dream." Jim paused, wondering if he should continue. And you were in it." Jim watched for Jonathan's reaction, but he got nothing; not a word, not even a raised eyebrow....nothing. So he continued, "The only reason I even bring that up is because you said the same thing in the dream."

"Actually, what I said was; 'If I'm interrupting your solitude, I can leave'."

Jim instantly felt hot, his hands clammy and beads of sweat formed on his forehead. He looked at Jonathan and there was no surprise on his face. "How the hell did you know that?" Jim asked.

First looking into his cup and then at Jim, he said, "How did you know my name was Jonathan?" His eyes now benevolently focused on Jim, waiting for his response.

"I never said it was your name. Well, not out loud, anyway."

"Maybe not, but you did know that's my name...right? So explain... please," Jonathan prodded.

Shrugging his shoulders, Jim said, "I must have caught it this morning when I looked at the sign-up board."

"I never signed in," Jonathan said with a half-grin and then continued. "Any other brilliant ideas?" he said, daring Jim to come up with a better explanation.

"How about a lucky guess? Or better yet, maybe you look like a Jonathan to me," Jim said with a chuckle.

Jonathan began to speak but stopped as if another thought had just entered his mind. He looked at Jim and said, "Wait a minute, what do you mean, I look like a Jonathan? What the hell does a Jonathan look like anyway?" He shook his head, waving his hand in front of him and said, "Never mind, I don't even want to go there right now. And to answer your question as to why I was in your dream, let's just say that there are many corridors of space-time and your dreams are simply one of them."

Jim's first thought was that this guy had been drinking long before he showed up with the load of wood for the fire, or maybe he was simply rambling. Jim decided to hear him out, mostly because at this point there was no polite way to just walk away. Besides, there was something intriguing about what he was posing and Jim hadn't had the opportunity for a good philosophical conversation in a long time. He hoped that this dialog could go in that direction.

Jim gave Jonathan a puzzled look that spoke volumes but couldn't resist asking, "Wow...where did that come from? I may be a bit drunk, but what the hell are you talking about?"

Jonathan paused, looked into his cup again and then grinned. "Why did I mention corridors of time-space, or why did we meet in your dream at all?"

Jim responded with, "Ok, let's start with *why meet in my dreams*?"

"Smart move; start with the easier question. The strange things that happen in dreams are much easier for people to accept. The same holds true for the cover of darkness. Why do you think they lower the lights in the movie theater? It's much easier to suspend disbelief in the dark... and the same goes for our dreams." He paused, looking at Jim inquisitively. "Aren't you at all curious to know *why* we have met?"

"What do you mean, *why* have we met? I don't even know if you are real."

"I assure you, I'm as real as you believe yourself to be."

"Well okay then, we meet people... because..." Jim hesitated, looking for a good answer. "We just meet people. It just happens; coincidence, destiny I guess," Jim said.

Jonathan began to laugh, a deep belly-shaking laugh. He caught himself, biting his lip when he saw Jim was serious. "Oh, I'm sorry," he said, wiping the tears from his eyes. "I thought you were trying to be funny. You *were* being funny, you know!" He chuckled under his breath a little more. "In a world in which coincidence and destiny rule, no personal voice can be possible. And you seriously believe this to be true? I, for a fact, know you don't think so...or we wouldn't be here right now."

Jonathan's statement made Jim uncomfortable and self-conscious. At this point Jim just wanted Jonathan to go away. He even thought about asking him to leave, but Jim didn't like confrontations and would feel awkward. Jim decided to quietly sit there and sip his drink and hope that maybe Jonathan would take the hint and depart of his own accord. But under the influence of the tequila, Jim couldn't resist and blurted out, "What's so funny about what I said? Are you telling me that the people we meet aren't random? If that is true, than my whole life is predestined, so why should I bother doing anything? I'll just sit here on my ass and wait for everybody and everything to come to me!" He paused for a moment proud of his response, but then words came out of his mouth as if someone else was speaking them. "Okay, so now you're going to say that we don't meet purely by accident, right?"

Jonathan cocked his head slightly in approval but said nothing. Jim continued as if he was 'channeling' the Dalai Lama, "What if who we meet IS predestined...and that's the key." Jim wasn't sure where his words were coming from but it somehow sounded right and he continued. "We determine our future by whom we choose to interact with, or not, and vice-versa...kind of an intermediate predestination."

Jonathan's face straightened. "You're getting warmer, but why are you and I here now?"

"We have a similar interest, skydiving, and *that* lead us to a common place like this drop zone."

"Similar interest, okay, I'll buy that to a point. Now this is starting to get interesting; keep going."

Jim looked at Jonathan, as if he had lost his thought.

Jonathan prompted him by asking, "Okay, why me and not someone else who spends time out here?"

"That's the destiny part," Jim said.

"Oh, you were so close! You've got the right idea; you've just got it bassakwards. You just got done saying it yourself; you don't have any choice in who you meet, just in what you choose to do with them. You were close, James. You were so damn close, I thought you had it. I really did!" Jonathan fell silent for a moment as he formulated his thoughts. "James, we can move mountains until we are taught that it can't be done. You've gotten too used to this world and its linear thinking." Jonathan's last statement surprised Jim and he fumbled for words but none came. He wanted to ask questions, but how could he respond to a statement like that?

Jonathan saw the look in Jim's eyes and spoke again, trying to help. "James, why did you put yourself here?"

"Maybe it's because you've got knowledge that I need to learn."

Jonathan fell silent for a moment and then asked, "Remember the door you saw in your dream?"

"Yeah, what about it?" Jim said. Finally, a familiar subject!

"We've met because of a choice you've made in the past."

"What does that have to do with me seeing some door in a dream? Why would that cause us to meet?"

"The door represents the choices you've made to date and those choices have led you to this very experience. The things you chose to do, the people you've befriended and those you've chosen to alienate have all contributed to this very moment. This is just one of the many possible outcomes. You are the product of all the choices you've made up to this moment. It's that simple."

45

"It is, huh? So where am I? I feel like I'm in a dream. Am I? That's it... isn't it? It's a lucid, 110 proof tequila-induced dream. After everyone else left tonight I got drunk, fell asleep by the fire and now I'm dreaming. Cool! It all makes sense now."

Jonathan gave him a disappointed look and then said, "If that's the case, don't wake up too fast. Let's start from the beginning...shall we?" He stood and walked off, disappearing completely into the shadows.

Jim reached for the bottle of tequila, thought of what had just transpired and opted to leave it alone. He didn't need any more help in misunderstanding this man. But then he decided it couldn't hurt and took a short gulp from the bottle. Jim wondered where Jonathan had ventured off to in the darkness as he set the bottle back down under his chair. Jonathan reappeared a minute later, grabbed a couple of chunks of firewood from the back of his truck and threw them on the fire.

"Where did you go?" Jim asked.

"It's not something that I thought I needed to announce, but if you really need to know, I took a piss," he said with a chuckle, as if he was amused with himself.

They drank in silence for a while, staring into the fire. The unanswered questions annoyed Jim and he finally asked sincerely, "So, why you are here?"

Still staring into the fire, Jonathan said, "You needed firewood....and I brought it to you."

"And?"

"And... apparently you're not ready for the rest of the answer."

"Try me," Jim said with conviction.

Jonathan leaned forward, looked at Jim as if he was judging his sincerity and hesitated as if he was second-guessing his decision to speak. "This universe is a machine that operates on people's perception of it. This is an undeniable truth and there are so many examples of it in our society. Our entire economy is based upon perceptions. Think of the stock market and our need for insurance policies. The stock market goes up on 'hopes' and down on 'fears.'. We buy insurance because we fear getting into an accident or being sued. Everything is based upon hope verses fear. Everything is how we think, and therefore feel about it. And those emotions mold our thoughts, which in turn create our reality." Jonathan paused and looked at Jim. "Are you following me here?"

Jim nodded, "I think so...keep going."

Jonathan continued, "Everything we have experienced, heard, read, observed makes up our reality. Now...take this one step further – verbalizing our thoughts solidifies our reality by reinforcing our thoughts and emotions, bringing it 'full circle.' Then all of our being is involved - as in Spirit (ourselves), Soul (our mind, will, and emotions), and Body (physical voice and hearing it with our ears). Or, as religion would say, Father, Son and Holy Spirit."

"What does that have to do with why we met?"

"Do you want to hear what I have to say, or do you want to debate?" Jonathan asked, his eyes piercing through Jim like blue lasers. Like a submissive dog, Jim tried not to look in the direction of Jonathan's gaze. "Maybe I was right; you're not ready to hear what I have to say," Jonathan said as if talking to himself.

"May I continue now?" Jonathan said rhetorically, still staring at Jim. "The universe is exactly as we choose to see it. We can see everything or nothing depending on our perspective. It's black or white or any shade of gray that we choose. We create all of the joy and drama we need in our quest to learn our lessons." He paused, making sure Jim understood what he was saying. Jim furled his brow, a natural reaction when he was processing a thought. Jonathan continued, "Let me put it another way. If a tree falls in the woods and you're not there to see it fall, *does the forest exist?*"

"Don't you mean, does it make a sound?"

Jonathan took a deep exaggerated breath and exhaled with a heavy sigh. "Would you please answer my question without asking one?"

"Of course it does."

"How do you know that?"

"You just told me it was there; where ever *'there'* is," he said, trying to lighten the moment.

47

"What if I lied?" Jonathan asked bluntly.

"I'm sorry, but I still don't understand what any of this has to do with why you're here."

Jonathan continued as if he hadn't even heard Jim. "Everything we know, we've learned from someone. We've learned from our mothers, our fathers, brothers and sisters, aunts and uncles, teachers, books. You get the idea? Who did these people learn from? Their mothers and fathers, brothers and sisters, aunts and uncles and so forth." He hesitated finally, taking a breath before continuing. "What I'm saying is that everything we know has been taught to us by someone who has been taught by someone before them…true?"

"Is this why we have met? I'm supposed to learn something?"

"You're jumping ahead. Answer my question first."

"Sure, that makes sense."

Jonathan's eyes lit up, his expression and body energized as he looked directly at Jim and slowly said, "What if 'they' were wrong? What if someone, way back whenever, made a poor observation or filled in a gap with either a misconception or a little white lie? It was done all the time; still is. Religions have done a great job of doing that very thing and gotten away with it for millennia. The Earth is the center of the universe...after all, who's going to know?" Jonathan questioned and continued.

"Everything you know may be based on a non-truth. Our reality is dependent upon what we choose to believe. Everything in our world hinges on the dramas we choose to participate in. It's all in how and what we choose to believe is real. Our reality can only extend to the edge of our knowledge. Nothing exists until we allow it to enter our consciousness."

"So what you are trying to tell me is this world is not seen by others the same way I see it?" Jim asked.

"Exactly… how could they? No one can see it as you do," he said matter-of-factly. A big smile came to his face. "And they said you wouldn't catch on. Okay, here it is: We live in a world of connect-the-dots. As you move from one dot to another you believe there is a purpose. You're not quite sure what the final picture is going to look like until you finish. Imagination is the key. Along the way you can imagine many different things, all of them potential results."

"Can you give me an example?"

"Absolutely not!" Jonathan said straight faced.

Jim's head snapped toward Jonathan. "WHAT?"

"I just wanted to see if you were really paying attention. Okay, here is an example, but then I'm done preaching. Did I sound like I was preaching? I hate it when I preach." He paused for a moment then continued without waiting for a response. "You've got a mechanical mind…you're the type who needs to see something for it to make sense, so I'll use some visuals."

"Visuals?"

"Visual flashcards if you will." He stood and motioned for Jim to follow him, "Come with me. You are capable of walking and talking at the same time aren't you? Just to be on the safe side, if you've got gum in your mouth; spit it out," he said with a slight chuckle in his voice. "And bring the bottle of tequila with you; we may need it."

"Where are we going?"

"You'll see. Trust me. The walk will do you some good and you might even enjoy the exercise."

They walked away from the warmth of the glowing fire and across the nicely groomed grass runway already covered with heavy dew. They jumped a small drainage ditch and continued into the neighboring hay field. Jim looked back, seeing the tiny flicker of fire still burning.

The coarse alfalfa stubble from last year's cutting crunched under his feet as they walked. Jim knew that Jonathan was barefoot and he couldn't imagine how Jonathan could walk on the stuff without it hurting his feet, but it apparently didn't seem to bother him. Three rectangular shapes came into view ahead of them, glowing in the reflective bluish-white light of the moon. As they walked closer, the blurry forms began to take on more detail. The rectangles were actually doors, much like the one Jim had seen in his dream. When they got about ten feet from the doors Jonathan held his hand out in front of Jim in a motion to stop. Jim stood beside Jonathan, completely puzzled.

"What are you thinking? You look confused," Jonathan said.

"I think I'm more surprised than confused."

Without looking at Jim, Jonathan said, "Pick one."

"That one, there," Jim said, pointing to the door on the far left. There was no thought, rhyme or reason to his choice.

Jonathan rolled his eyes in disbelief and then in a deep commanding voice he said, "Luke...feel the force, Luke."

"What?" Jim asked, again wrinkling his brow.

"It's something from a Star Wars movie. It seemed dramatic and I thought it fit the situation."

Jim continued to look at him oddly.

"Well, it worked in the movie," Jonathan said. He shrugged his shoulders and smiled, "I was wrong, so shoot me." The smile then fell from his face and he looked more serious. "Okay, now back to the task at hand. Feel the doors, sense them the same way you feel an airplane when you're flying. Feel it in your gut. Let your intuition guide you. Feel it down on that level where all is known. When you feel what you are doing is right, you know you can't go wrong." Then he added. "Listen to that little voice inside even when your mind tries to override it."

Jim reached out for the first door, but before he even touched it, his stomach began to churn. He felt nauseous to the point of nearly vomiting. Jim pulled his hand back quickly and looked at Jonathan for some kind of direction. Jonathan stood there, expressionless.

"What's behind this door?" Jim asked.

"Open it and find out," Jonathan dared.

"I think not!" Again, looking at Jonathan for direction, Jim shrugged, "I don't understand any of this."

"For God's sake, pretend you are on The Price is Right, and pick a door."

"What's the significance?"

"James, quit thinking so much right now. What is your gut instinct telling you?"

Jim turned back to the doors and put his hand near the second door. This one didn't make him sick as he reached for it like the first one did. Instead it left him feeling sad, a sense of emptiness. It was cold and didn't feel right. Jim reached out for the third door not knowing what to expect. This door gave him a sense of warmth and invitation. He felt a grin on his face and he knew this was the one. For whatever reason, he knew this door was the one he was supposed to choose. Jim pointed to the door with the exaggerated smile of a child taking his first unassisted steps and nodded to Jonathan, "This one! This one is my pick." Then he began to laugh.

"What's so funny?" Jonathan asked.

"I feel like Goldilocks and the three doors," Jim said. He walked around the doors but found nothing. Where the other side of the doors should have been, he saw only alfalfa stubble and Jonathan looking back at him. The hay field met a beautiful night sky complete with a full moon and an array of stars. Jonathan's face beamed as he saw the bewildered look on Jim's. Jim walked back over and stood next to Jonathan. He turned around, and there once again, were the doors. Neither of them said a word.

Jim realized that he hadn't physically touched any of them yet, and he now thought they may have been some sort of illusion or hologram. He reached out to touch one of them, expecting his hand to pass through some invisible curtain, but instead hit the solid surface of a real door. He ran his hand across it and it was solid.

Looking at Jonathan, he motioned back to the door, "May I?"

A grin broke across Jonathan's face as he nodded. Jim grabbed the knob, gave it a twist and pushed on the door but it didn't open. He pulled this time and it still didn't move. "What the Hell? It's stuck."

"It's not stuck, it's locked," Jonathan quipped.

"It's LOCKED? Is this some kind of joke? It's just a one-sided, two-dimensional door in the middle of a big empty field; why would it be locked?"

"Seek and you shall find. Knock and doors will be opened to you. Do you know who said that?"

"You just did," Jim said.

51

"No, I mean the first time."

"I only heard it once, and you said it," Jim said, deliberately trying to annoy Jonathan.

Jonathan rolled his eyes and threw his hands into the air. "Forget it," he said, then he added, "It was Jesus, damn it! It was Jesus!"

Jim flashed him a smile. Jonathan knew instantly that Jim had gotten the better of him this time. "You are a quick study my boy," he said. Jim turned back to the door of his choice and knocked on it, giving it three firm but soft raps and said, *"Open sesame!"* He turned the knob and pulled the door open toward himself as he looked back at Jonathan. While still looking at Jonathan, Jim took a step toward the threshold. He asked Jonathan, "How do I look?"

"Pretty stupid. And watch your step; the first one is a big one," he said. Jim turned back only to realize he was about to take a *ten thousand-foot* step... straight down!

Jim lurched back, his stomach flip-flopping as he fell backward onto his butt. He righted himself and crawled on his hands and knees, inching his way back over to the threshold. The view was amazing. It was daylight, about mid-morning as far as he could tell. Jim recognized the surroundings below immediately. They were directly over the drop zone.

"I'm so confused," Jim said. "This wasn't at all what I was expecting."

"I'm sure it wasn't," Jonathan replied.

"That's got to be a ten thousand foot drop."

"Give or take a little. You're a good judge of distance."

"Thanks, it comes with being a pilot, I guess. But how do these doors and stuff work?"

"I haven't the faintest idea, but they're here."

"What do you mean; you don't have the faintest idea? You're the one who dragged me out here. You set up this whole *'visual flashcard'*, as you called it, and now you're telling me you don't know?" Jim thought Jonathan was just being coy once again and not being totally forthcoming.

"That's right," he said with a grin. "There are even greater imaginations than we can comprehend. We can only use what we are given and channel it as best we can." It seemed as if he could somehow guide events but didn't have complete control over them. He changed the subject by saying, "Let's take advantage of the situation."

"What do you mean?" Jim asked.

"Let's jump. It would be a shame to waste the opportunity."

Jim suddenly felt like a teenager with the keys to his parents' car. This was fantastic. If this was a dream, he didn't care and at this moment, didn't want to wake up. He didn't want to think about what was happening. He was afraid that if he thought about it too much, it would somehow make it all vanish.

Jim began walking in the direction of the hanger when Jonathan stopped him by saying, "Where are you running off to... I thought you wanted to jump?"

"To get my jumping rig and gear from the locker. We're going to need it if we're going to jump. Are you coming?"

"You don't need any of that stuff."

"I beg your pardon? Didn't you just say that you wanted to make a jump?"

"Yes, but you won't be needing a chute," Jonathan said. Through the darkness, Jim could see Jonathan's eyes had changed color again and were now glowing blue.

"I don't understand. Did you think I'd just step out that doorway without a chute? If you did, you are sadly mistaken...if not completely crazy!"

"My mental status has nothing to do with it. It's a leap of faith. All important choices are, of course!"

"And you honestly expect me just to hurl my body out of a doorway at ten thousand feet, give or take a little, because you said I should."

Without a word, Jonathan bolted past Jim as he leapt through the doorway and disappeared from view. Jim rushed to the doorway and looked down expecting to see Jonathan free-falling, but he wasn't. He looked left and then right, scouring the area for him, but still no Jonathan.

"Are you looking for me?" a voice asked from the space in front of Jim.

Jim looked up slightly to find Jonathan sitting in a cross-legged lotus position, floating in mid-air with a big smile on his face. He hovered there as if he were in the middle of some sort of Hollywood special effects sound stage.

"What the hell?"

"You spend way too much time arguing your limitations, James," he said.

"How do you do this stuff?"

"Simply make a choice, any choice, believe it to be true and it will be. It's like making up a true story. But why should I have all the fun? Come on in here!"

"What do you mean, come on in here? Shouldn't it be, out here?"

"Once again, it depends on your perspective...now, doesn't it?"

"Leap of faith, huh? Believe it to be true and it will be, huh?" Jim wanted to prove something to Jonathan; besides, he was convinced that this was some sort of dream and figured he could wake himself up if he started to fall. He closed his eyes, pictured an invisible bridge and stepped out onto it. He heard Jonathan giggle. As he stood there afraid to open his eyes, Jim asked, "Did I make it?"

"Make what? If you mean through the doorway, the answer is, yes you did. I bet you're full of yourself right about now, aren't you?"

Jim opened his eyes and realized he was standing in mid-air, supported by nothing. He kicked his heels down on the invisible hardness, making a clunking noise. Bits of encrusted dirt fell from his high-top sneakers and continued falling out of sight. He had a spooky feeling this wasn't just a dream, and that feeling suddenly turned to fear. Jim's breathing became tight and difficult. He turned to retreat toward the doorway as the sky below him gave way. The tinny taste of adrenaline filled his mouth as he frantically reached for the doorway, only to have his outstretched fingertips graze past the bottom of the threshold.

He watched as the doorway diminished in size. He was falling. He tumbled in a terrified panic, screaming as he fell. "Jonathan!" He thought to himself, *wake up, wake up!*

His skydiving instincts took over; his arms and legs went out, his chest arched forward stabilizing his fall in a typical face down freefall position. Jim was only buying time as he wondered, 'now what?' It was then he noticed Jonathan was free falling beside him. He looked at Jim with a calm in his eyes that was reassuring, and Jim was no longer afraid. Jonathan yelled out, "James, I can't save you. You must save yourself. Remember to make it real and don't make it harder than it needs to be."

To that Jim said, "Thanks a lot… Shit head!"

Jonathan smiled and said, "There is something you need to know in this world: Find your footing or learn how to fly."

Suddenly everything slowed to a near stop. Jim rotated into a heads-up position as if his invisible chute had opened and he was under canopy. Jim's feet swung under him and he instinctively reached above his head to release the steering toggles, but there were none. He looked over and saw Jonathan just feet away from him, but neither said a word, although Jonathan was wearing the content expression on his face of a proud parent. It felt odd not having something in his hands to grasp or to control his turns. Jim became very self-conscious of his hands, not knowing what to do with them. He finally folded them across his chest and wondered how he was going to turn. He thought of turning to the right and he began spinning to the right at a rate he expected. When he wanted to go left, the same thing happened to the left. It was great! They turned and twisted for what seemed like an hour until they finally touched solid ground with a gentle landing. As they walked towards the hanger Jim knew that it wasn't a dream, but at the same time, not quite sure if any of it was real either. He may have been numb or in shock but he didn't think any of this as odd or strange; it was just something that was happening.

"Now, how do we get back?" Jim asked.

"Get back where?" Jonathan asked with a puzzled expression on his face.

"To the drop zone."

"You're at the drop zone. Same place, just a different perspective." He continued, "This is an alternate choice. If you had chosen one of the other doors and stepped through, you'd be somewhere or sometime else."

Everything still looked the same to Jim, but somehow everything felt different. In his mind it was supposed to be night time. It was as if the whole world had been tilted slightly. He was uncomfortable and wanted to go back to the night-time drop-zone they had left. He was getting anxious; his stomach was queasy and knotted. "You mean we can't go back?"

"You are back. You never left!"

"But it's light out, it wasn't when we left. This just feels weird."

"Ah, don't do this to me," Jonathan moaned. "Don't be like everyone else and see the world in terms of what you expect to see and not what it actually is. You're not in a strange place, just different than what you were expecting. You've already experienced this place, just perceiving it differently. You need to remember this!"

Jim just looked at him, almost in tears.

"Okay, okay, if you'll quit your whining and stop looking at me like that, we'll cheat a little.... follow me."

Jonathan led Jim toward the small storage closet in the back of the hanger where the club members stored their jumpsuits, canopy rigs and personal gear. Jonathan motioned with his index finger for Jim to follow him into the closet.

"Where we going, Jonathan? There's not enough room for both of us in there. There's barely enough room in there for all our crap as it is. Why would you want me to follow you in there anyway? Come on, I just want to go home!"

"What did I tell you about your whining? Just follow me!" Jonathan said commandingly, having lost his patience and obviously annoyed with Jim's apprehension.

They entered the closet, moving slowly, groping through the darkness. Jim carefully shuffled his feet forward, doing a *Frankenstein* kind of thing with his arms in front of him. He knew the storage closet was only eight feet deep and they had already ventured further than that into the darkness. As his eyes began to adjust to the darkness, a glowing night-light came into view. Jim realized they were no longer in the storage closet, but under a canopy of stars; and what he thought was the night-light was actually the moon. He took a sigh of relief with the sudden return to what he felt was normalcy. He felt like he was finally back under the same starlit sky he had left earlier. The moon was full and the fire was still burning. Jim was comforted by the fact that he was home.

They walked back to the fire and sat in silence for some time. Jim wasn't sure if what he had just experienced had been real or some kind of hypnosis or hallucination. All he knew was that it was a damp, chilly night with a beautifully clear sky and that the warmth of the fire felt good on his body. They both stared contently into the fire.

Jonathan broke the silence. "Did our little adventure teach you anything?" he asked, without looking away from the glow of the fire.

"I think so, but I'm not sure I can put it into words yet," Jim said, trying to formulate what was in his head. The sensory overload left him speechless. Too much was rushing through his head to try to process it all into something coherent enough that he could talk about. Finally he just said, "Thanks, Jonathan."

"Thanks for what?"

"The visual. I think I'm beginning to understand how all my choices in my life have brought me to this moment in time.... *this NOW*. But I don't understand what difference it makes, *right now*."

"Can you change it?"

"I don't have a frickin' clue right now. If you don't mind, I'm tired and I don't think I can handle any more questions tonight. I think I need to sleep. Do you know what I mean?"

"Yes I do James. We'll talk more later, but take one thing with you tonight. Remember that *the secret is that everyone knows*."

"Yeah...alright," Jim replied automatically, without really thinking of what Jonathan had just said. "And thanks," Jim mumbled. They sat in silence for some time; neither of them moved. Then Jim asked him, "In the dream I had earlier on the picnic table…you said that it was time again. Time again for what?"

Jonathan grinned to himself as he let out a barely audible snort. He knew Jim had enough going on in his head without piling on more. He simply said, "Say good night, Gracie."

Jim mumbled, "Good night Gracie."

Chapter 6
The Powers

As the vision faded and reality returned, Jim and Rabina found themselves once again in the same positions they had started, but this time they were engulfed in a faint glow of golden light. Rabina was the first to speak, "Wow, I'm glowing...cool!" She then looked at Jim and asked, "Is that where you got the idea for our 'visual' back at the quarry? Did Jonathan teach you how to do that?"

"To tell you the truth, I hadn't thought about it at the time...at least not on a conscious level. And no, Jonathan didn't teach me anything like that," Jim answered. Rabina was busy moving her arms around, looking at the light surrounding her. "Look at us...we're glowing! Is this normal?"

Jim laughed. "See what I mean? You're thinking that this could be considered normal already. This glow IS pretty cool, but a little eerie as well."

"I just think it's cool," Rabina said, admiring the glow as she moved her arm up and down, following it with her eyes. "Jim, why did you start the 'vision' when Mark and Lisa showed up at the zone instead of later, when Jonathan showed up with the wood?"

"I didn't start anything anywhere...I just closed my eyes and took the ride with you. I don't have a clue as to how that all works."

"Wow, I'd like to know how that works! I'd love to bottle it. I'd make a fortune with it on eBay," she said dreamily, and then changed the subject. "So what happened next?"

"I went to sleep."

"What?" Rabina said, surprised.

"I was tired."

"Well, where did Jonathan go?"

"I don't know."

"What do you mean, you don't know?"

"You've got to understand I was so drained after all that, I left him sitting by the fire and I went up to the hanger, crawled into my sleeping bag and crashed. At least I think that's what happened...I was that tired."

"You've got to be kidding me! You just went to sleep after what had happened?"

"I was exhausted, mentally as well as physically. I was so burned out from everything that had happened. I'm sure the tequila didn't help either, but I couldn't keep my eyes opened any more. I needed to sleep!"

Rabina asked, "So when did it all start to sink in?"

Jim paused, thinking for a moment and then answered, "Well, I was pretty much dead to the world, metaphorically speaking that is, until the next morning when the damn crows woke me up with their incessant cawing. I thought it was way too early for them to be making noise. It was that time of the morning when things start transitioning from shades of gray to color. You know what I mean?"

Rabina nodded with a grin, "Are you aware that you just gave the definition of dawn? Don't get me wrong...it was a great description anyway. You should be writing some of this stuff down. You're really pretty good at putting me right there in the middle of it."

"Thanks, I have been jotting down a few notes along the way...actually, a lot of notes," Jim answered, pleased with himself. "Now you made me self-conscious. Where was I?" He paused, ready to continue his story, "Oh yeah, the birds were there to scavenge whatever scraps people had dropped on the ground from lunch the day before. I didn't appreciate them being around so damn early, especially considering how my head felt. I laid there in my sleeping bag, not wanting to move because my head was pounding. I hadn't had enough sleep and my mind was fuzzy from all that tequila. But as my head began to clear, I started remembering things that had happened the night before. I knew I should write down as much as I could before I forgot the details. My brain was willing but my body still didn't really want to move. Once I finally got enough ambition to roll out of the sleeping bag and off the couch, I grabbed my spiral binder, flipped it open to an empty page and started outlining what had happened the night before. Once I started writing, details kept coming to me, so I kept writing. It was as if I couldn't stop. The pen just kept moving in my hand and the words kept filling page after page in my binder. The more I wrote, more details fell into place. It became so simple and clear. That was, until I remembered the last thing Jonathan had said to me that night. It was that comment about, *'The secret is that everyone knows'*. That I didn't understand…everyone knows *what*?"

Rabina interrupted, "What do you think he meant by that?"

"Like I said, I don't know. When I looked out by the fire pit, Jonathan and his truck were gone. I wasn't surprised, but I really wanted to talk to Jonathan again. I couldn't wait to sit down with him over a cup of coffee somewhere and rehash what had happened the night before to find out *how* he made those things happen. Jonathan's line about *'the secret that everyone knows'* kept rattling around in my head along with the Pink Floyd tune, *Just Another Brick in the Wall*.

Every time the door of the hanger swung opened that morning I hoped it was him. By 9:30 I began to think that he might not show. We had enough pilots that day, so I didn't have to fly. After what I had had to drink the night before, that was a good thing. But I knew I was also ready to start making a few more jumps again."

Rabina stopped him, "I remember; I was a little surprised when you mentioned making a jump with me. It was the first time in a long time that you really wanted to get out and jump. You never really seemed comfortable sitting on the floor behind the pilot in the plane, were you?"

"That's a whole 'nother story I'll tell you some other time…okay? Anyway, back to my story."

"Sorry, I didn't mean to interrupt. Go on," Rabina said with a smile. She waved her hand, prompting him to continue.

Jim smiled back, "As I was saying, I wanted to tell everyone about what had happened, but I knew it was so over-the-top that I wanted Jonathan there to corroborate my story. So while I waited for him to show up, I paced around the hanger and the rest of the drop zone not knowing what to do with myself, hoping Jonathan's little truck would pull up, but that didn't happen.

The only thing that could have brightened my day at that point would have been if the strawberry blonde had shown up to distract me again. At one point I was sure I heard the distinct sound of Jonathan's rotted-out exhaust system pulling into the parking lot, but it was just someone in an old brown rusted beater-car.

I finally decided to quit waiting for Jonathan to show up and make the most of the day. That's when I asked you and Dana if you would make a jump with me."

"That was the time you took the digger into the ground...right?"

"Yeah, and none of you ever let me forget it either. I thought I had enough altitude when I cranked on that toggle and spun around, but it just kinda fell away on me. Man...when my feet caught the turf...did I take a digger! I flipped over and landed flat on my back so hard that it knocked the wind out of me. I couldn't breathe for a minute or so, but the worst thing was the bruising my ego took. I was more embarrassed than actually hurt. I knew I was laying there because I was rusty...and being a *hotdog*. There's nothing worse than an old rusty hotdog.

I eventually got up, brushed myself off, gathered up my canopy along with what was left of my dignity and walked slowly toward the hanger. With my tail still firmly between my legs, I was met with a stirring round of applause from everyone that saw it happen. That was when you sailed overhead and yelled something. I couldn't tell what you said but I knew it was in reference to my landing. And then you had the audacity to go and make such a graceful landing...you pissed me off! You never did tell me what you had yelled that day."

"If I remember correctly, I think I just asked if you were okay," she said with a grin.

"Yeah, and I'm the tooth fairy!" Jim said with a chuckle. "Jonathan never did show up, and on the drive home I started to second guess myself as to if anything that I remembered from the night before had actually happened. I wasn't even sure if Jonathan was ever there...maybe it had just been a dream. Everything had been so vivid when it happened, but by the end of the day I wasn't so sure. It seemed less real and more dreamlike. The memory was still there but the emotional connection was gone. It was kinda like running into an old flame after you've moved on with your life. You have memories of the person but the emotional connection you once had just isn't there anymore."

"Yeah, I know exactly what you mean," Rabina said. She nodded her head and then asked, "So did you actually make the jump and skydive from the doorway?"

"I think so, but it doesn't really matter. I'm learning that it's more about your perception of what happened that makes an event your own. Do you want to hear the rest of the story now, or are your interruptions an attempt to stop me long enough so you can get another drink?" Jim asked with a half-grin.

"Oh, yeah I want you to continue, but since you mention it, my throat is getting kinda dry. Since you insist, I will have another glass of wine...just to make you happy," Rabina replied with a wink.

Not wanting to be chastised for being stingy again, Jim poured until her glass was nearly full. Rabina gave him a thumbs-up and a nod of approval saying, "Now that's what I call a glass of wine!"

Jim continued his story as he placed the box of wine back on the table close to Rabina. "When I got home I dragged my aching body, which felt old and bruised after my little miscalculation on that landing, into the house and grabbed a bottle of beer from the crisper drawer of the refrigerator. On my way to the kitchen table I grabbed a bottle of aspirin to go with my beer. I figured that I could minimize my aches and pains by keeping myself medicated.

I had a couple more beers and a few more aspirin, then headed for the comfort of my bed. I dropped my blue jeans and shirt on the floor by the bed. It felt wonderful to crawl into the most comfortable bed I've ever owned. As I was drifting off to sleep, I couldn't stop thinking about that strawberry blonde. I wanted another chance to meet her; not that I had actually met her, but I promised myself that next time I got the chance I would have the courage to talk to her. That's what I love about those dreamy thoughts as you're falling asleep; anything is possible!

The next thing I knew I was sitting in that damn little yellow inflatable boat. It was the first time I experienced that place in the abyss. At least it was the first time I remembered being there. I opened my eyes to see that deep aquamarine color. There was an eerie tension in the air that seemed to be screaming out in the silence.

An expensive double bladed carbon-fiber kayak paddle was nestled next to me. I wanted to paddle somewhere but I didn't have a clue as to what direction I should go. There wasn't any sign of land anywhere, just water. As a pilot, I instinctively looked to the sky for some navigational reference point. There was nothing. The North Star was nowhere to be found. There weren't any familiar stars anywhere in the sky, just a jumbled mess of tiny lights and they all seemed to be moving. None of it made sense at the time.

I sat there with the paddle across my lap, paralyzed with indecision. I knew that I'd only compound my problems and make matters worse if I were to paddle in the wrong direction.

In the dim light, the sky blended seamlessly with the water and that aquamarine color made it impossible to differentiate between the two of them. I felt as if I was in a bubble without a horizon; just a continuous unending curve. The area was devoid of any breeze and the silence around me was deafening and unnatural. It was frightening.

My heart was pounding in my throat and I was trying to fight off the panic. That place, like Jonathan, was familiar but I just didn't remember how. There was a sense that I had been there before and that was spooky in itself.

The silence was broken by the slow cadence of a paddle leisurely breaking the water. There was someone out there and I yelled out hoping whoever it was would hear me. But the only sound was that of the paddle. I yelled again and this time I thought I heard the sound of someone whistling somewhere in the distance. I wasn't sure if I was hearing right, but when I listened closer I couldn't believe that someone out there was actually whistling *'Row, row, row your boat'*. Can you believe that? I called out again as the whistling moved closer. There was some sense of relief knowing I wasn't out there alone. Anything was better than the eerie silence, and for some reason I was pretty sure the whistler was going to be Jonathan.

A red canoe came into sight and I was relieved when I saw that it was indeed Jonathan.

He came along side my raft and smiled. The boats were now side by side and we faced each other."

"Where were you today?" I asked.

"You should have listened to those crows this morning. They were telling you that I had other things to do."

I figured this was his way of telling me it was none of my business to know where he had been, so I dropped the subject.

Jonathan looked around and said, "Beautiful night to be out, isn't it?" But before I could answer, he continued with a slightly puzzled look on his face, "Why did you bring me out here?"

"ME? I didn't bring you here. I went to sleep in my own bed and woke up here!" I said somewhat defensively.

"So this is one of your manifestations then...pretty cool," Jonathan said, nodding his head as if it somehow made sense to him.

"Seriously...my manifestation? This is another one of those manifestations? And I created it?"

"I think so."

"What do you mean, 'you think so'?"

"The universe presents itself to us in ways that we can perceive it. It's not always easy to distinguish reality and imagination... they have a tendency to blend together. It doesn't really matter," he replied with a distracted expression on his face, his mind obviously elsewhere. He sat quietly for just a moment and then turned his head toward me as if he had just finished a thought.

"There aren't any doors to choose this time, so why are you adrift out here, my boy?" he asked.

"I don't need more questions right now. I need answers."

"But this IS your answer."

"Excuse me?"

"Don't you see? This is exactly why you are here. It's obvious, you're troubled by something and that has put you here afloat...with me, nonetheless. The 'Powers-that-Be' are at it again, so let them help." he said, shrugging his shoulders.

"What are you talking about?"

Jonathan thought for a moment, as if he was choosing his words carefully before he spoke. "We are all put here to learn more about *who we are,* and there are things we need to experience to help us achieve that end. Some lessons are easy and we whiz right through them, while others are more covert, shrouded under layers of distraction, misdirection and temptation. But we need to experience those lessons before we can advance to the next lesson in our quest to finding our higher self."

"Kinda like the doors last night?" I asked.

Jonathan just nodded.

"What happens if we're not ready to learn the lesson presented to us?"

"That's the great thing about all this; you're never given a lesson that you haven't asked for or are incapable of learning. There's no sense in teaching algebra to a second grader. They need to learn the basics of simple math before they can grasp more complex problems."

"So who decides what I need to learn?"

"You do... well, to a degree. There's a level of consciousness where you...along with 'The Powers', decide when and what you are ready to experience. We know this on a *gut instinct* level if we are listening. That's not to say the Powers don't lead us in a direction when we need it."

"What if we refuse to learn?"

"That's your option. You're not obligated to do anything, but there is always a trade-off. Do you want to stay in second grade for the rest of your life? Emerson said, "Growth is the only sign of life." Without these experiences, you don't get the chance for any personal growth and you will exist in a cycle of recurring thoughts and events. But, as I said, there are times when the *'Powers'* within us give us choices designed to move us forward and put us where we need to be."

"Can you give me an example?"

"They led you to Josie's back porch three years ago, didn't they?"

"Yeah, I'd have to agree with you there. I've always said it was as if I had no choice but to meet her and to learn to fly."

"And *They've* put you right here, right now."

"Wow! You know Josie?" Jim asked, after that fact had sunk in.

"You shouldn't be surprised by the things we know. But that's not the point right now."

"OK then; what happens if we don't make the correct choices?" Jim asked.

"There's no real right or wrong choice. The worst that can happen is that you have to repeat the experiences, with subtle variations, until you have the answers you seek."

"Kind of like doing second grade until we learn our multiplication tables, huh?"

"You got it...remember, you can't learn algebra without understanding simple math."

"What happens if we still don't get it?"

"If it's important enough, *They,* being the '*Powers*,' will get through to you one way or another and *They* can get very creative when they choose to be. Things can sometimes escalate to a point where you can't avoid it any longer; *They* will give you a definite wake-up call."

"Like what?"

"Some people need a *significant emotional event*...something that brings them to the very edge before they '*see*' the lesson before them. Some people need a heart attack or a car crash or some sort of significant emotional event to find out where they need to be! But that's more the exception than the rule," he said without hesitation. "If you don't pay attention to your personal journey it will take you down a path of least resistance. You may simply follow the crowd and end up not having a clue as to who you are because you weren't paying attention to how you got there."

"So I should never follow the crowd?"

"Following the crowd is fine, if you choose to forget how easy it is to remember what we know from our past. Carl Jung, the Swiss psychiatrist, considered the process of separating ourselves from the crowd and focusing on being an individual necessary in becoming whole. Follow the signposts that will direct you on your own path. You are free to experience everything the way you choose to *have* the experience."

"Ok, what happens when we accept our experience?"

"You grow closer to who you are…and move on."

"To the next experience?"

"Yep!"

"So you're saying that we're given new experiences until we die."

"As you understand death, yeah, but then there are always other planes of existence to experience."

"Should we ever be satisfied with what we have experienced?"

"Of course…for a while. It's like climbing a mountain. You plan and prepare and then put your plan in motion by beginning the climb by putting one foot in front of the other. At some point you need a break, so you take a well-needed and deserved rest. You relax and enjoy the view from where you are sitting, but then you start looking over your shoulder at the next ascent. You want more…it's in your nature…and along the way you will find *God*."

"I didn't know how to even respond to that statement," Jim said to Rabina. He shrugged his shoulders and then continued. "Jonathan and I sat in silence for a moment, both of us caught up in our own thoughts. Then I asked him, "What really happened last night? It definitely was an *experience,* but what was the lesson?"

"James, we are to learn something from everything we do and everyone we meet. What you learn from an experience is up to you and is yours to keep or to let go of."

"Was it a dream, or did it really happen?"

"Does it really matter? The experience was real to you, so learn from it," he said, pausing with a look on his face that told me he was going to continue. "What is real or imagined is all relative to your perspective. We feel perfectly at rest on this seemingly stationary Earth and yet we know that it is spinning and orbiting the sun and all of that is swirling in the Milky Way at a bazillion miles per second. The same is true with everyday events. People can experience the same event and come away with very different realities from it. What one person may see the experience as a revelation, another may see it as worthless, and yet others see nothing at all. It all depends on the lesson plan we have set for ourselves and the choices we make."

Rabina looked at Jim and said, "Wow! That's really some deep stuff. I hope you wrote that down, because it's not easy to grasp in one sitting."

"Believe me, I've been writing as much as I can remember. It is hard to grasp at first and I don't always understand the stuff as it's happening...but writing it down seems to help. And it just keeps coming."

"I'm sorry...I didn't mean to interrupt your story, but I find it all so fascinating."

"Not a problem, I should take a break and see how the steaks are doing anyway." He got up, walked over to the grill and flipped the steaks with a sizzle and then he turned off the grill.

"How are they lookin'?"

"They're almost done...They need to rest, if you like them on the rare side. Now where was I?"

"You were talking about the lessons we choose to accept."

Jim continued, "Oh yeah, thanks. So then Jonathan said that the new experiences either strengthened your belief in *who you are* or help collapse the facade we've created for ourselves. What we take from any new experience helps define how we see this reality and our place in it. I asked him to give me another example."

"I'll give you two. The most obvious to me are Moby Dick and puberty." He said.

"MOBY DICK?" I asked

"Yes, Moby Dick," he said emphatically. "Most people who have read the book think of the classic as a long boring story about a man obsessed with killing a whale...that also happens to be my opinion, by the way...while others see it as great literature; a masterpiece. It's your choice, but whatever your opinion, it should make you think. It was the first book that ever dealt with the metaphor of human struggle within himself. Nothing had ever been written like that before. We tend to be impressed with a fresh thought. Sometimes it forces us to change our views and sometimes even stimulates us into action."

"Okay, now explain how puberty fits into this," I asked.

"Puberty is probably the biggest paradigm shift we experience in this reality. Before puberty, life is pretty simple. As a child, our biggest concerns are satisfied by a kiss on the top of our head from our mother."

"What is so bad about that?" I asked.

"Nothing, if you are satisfied remaining a child. But the wonderful experience of sexuality shifts our thought process to grander, more complex emotions. We are forced to look at the opposite sex with a whole different perspective and appreciation. When we pass into adolescence, we no longer see the opposite sex as having *cooties*."

"OK, but what are we supposed to learn from these lessons?"

"Once again, that is your choice. In puberty, you can choose to see the world from a new perspective…to embrace the newly discovered feelings you have for love and sex or you can deny yourself these new emotions…or anything else you choose to experience. Yet again, let me emphasize, it is your choice. Notice a pattern here? The main thing is to experience it and learn who you are once again and maybe adjust your path." He paused for a second and then asked, "Why do you think you were led to become a pilot?"

"I've thought about that. I had trouble enjoying the whole skydiving experience because I didn't like the plane ride. I hate to admit it, but it scared me."

"Why was that so important for you?"

"I'm a control freak when it comes to my survival. I feel much safer when I know what the plane…and more importantly, the pilot, is doing."

"Has becoming a pilot changed that feeling?"

I nodded *yes*.

Jonathan thought for a second and then asked, "So what you are telling me is that you learned to fly only to enjoy skydiving more?"

I nodded again, but cautiously. I could tell by the tone in his voice he was baiting me. There was an uncomfortable silence as Jonathan expected me to continue, but we sat in silence.

"And?" Jonathan finally prompted me.

"And what?" I asked.

He looked at me in disbelief. 'You spent all those hours in a tiny little airplane, shoulder to shoulder with Josie becoming a pilot and that's all you learned?"

"I always considered learning to fly was a pretty big deal."

Jonathan still shaking his head said, "It amazes me you haven't crashed yet. The Powers-that-Be must really like you. You're lucky we are sitting here afloat in this abyss instead of in a stalled plane somewhere spiraling out of control toward earth." He said those words with such conviction that it sent shivers through my entire body.

"What do you mean? I'm a damn good pilot!" I said defensively.

"James, being good has nothing whatsoever to do with it! Learning to fly was only a residual benefit of your experience. The real lessons go so much deeper than that."

I felt like I was being scolded. "You seem to be on a mission to teach me something here, so please teach. Come on, shower me with your gift of infinite wisdom," I said indignantly.

Unfazed, Jonathan said, "I'm not so much a teacher; I'm more of a reminder. Actually, a *guide* would be a more appropriate term. Don't forget, I've got lessons and experiences I'm working on too."

"Well okay, *Guide*; tell me what lessons I've learned from that experience besides how to fly an airplane?"

"That would be like letting you cheat off of my test paper...the WRONG test paper. You're going to have to find your own answers to your own questions from your own experiences and those answers can only come from within." Jonathan paused and then shrugged his shoulders and said, "Ah, what the hell, I'll throw you a bone and give you a hint that might help get you started down the right road here... Do you recall a conversation you had with Josie the day you met? The one about her friend who died in a plane crash just days before?"

"Yeah, what about it?"

"She gave you a great analogy of how the Powers-that-Be work."

"She did?"

"Yes, she did. Think about it."

"I just remember her telling me about how a close friend had crashed his plane on final approach just short of the runway at the local airport."

"Exactly!"

"Exactly?"

"Do you recall the details of that conversation?"

"I remember she felt bad about what had happened to her friend. She said he was a good pilot, and that he and his wife were planning to fly down to Florida later that same week. She also said he had gone out to the airport to practice a few instrument approaches before taking the trip."

"Go on," Jonathan prompted.

"Well, she said it just must have been his time to die."

"How so?"

"She thought there were too many little things that had gone wrong that day to be just coincidence. First, an ice-producing cold front moved into the area much sooner than was predicted. Next, he missed his first approach, which he never missed. That would have put him on the ground safely. Instead he had to go around."

"And?" Jonathan prompted again, waiting for Jim to see what was unfolding.

"After missing that approach he lost his electrical system, which included the radios, cockpit lights and some instruments. Then he had not one, but two flashlights malfunction on him. Finally, the ice loaded up on his wings and he just couldn't keep it in the air any longer. He nosed it in about a quarter of a mile short of the runway."

"And what bit of advice did she give you?"

"She told me to be aware of when you make a mistake, and to correct it as soon as possible. She said making one mistake while flying wouldn't kill you, and the second mistake usually wouldn't kill you either, but after that, things will start to escalate and the third, fourth and fifth mistakes will be right on their heels...and *they can and most probably will kill you.*"

"There you go...a very good, though not perfect, explanation of how the 'Powers' work."

"It is?"

"It says that you have to pay attention! It goes back to your question about what happens if we still don't get it. The 'Powers' find ways to get our attention. Sometimes the only way *They* get through to us is to escalate the intensity and frequency of the *'wake-up call'* until we finally get it!"

"But he died!"

"I didn't say that it was a perfect example. I'm just saying it's AN example."

There was a moment of silence as we both thought about things and then Jonathan said, "James, take an honest look at yourself and you'll find your answers. Look past the obvious. Look past all the interference. When you drive a car, you're used to seeing the world in terms of speed and distance. Flying forced you to think in three dimensions by adding altitude to the mix...and removing the brakes. The skydiving aspect aside, the view from the airplane window alone should change your perspective of the world. Think of all the things that you learned and shared with Josie. Use your past experiences to help you."

He waited, letting what he had said sink in and then added, "You have to realize that there is much more in your experiences than you are aware of." He leaned back against the plastic seat molded into his canoe, smiled a big smile and said, "We've gotten off the subject. What was your question again?"

"Why are we here?"

"Oh yes, that's an age-old question, James."

"STOP right there! I don't need you to ramble on for another hour about the meaning of life. Why are we afloat, HERE...NOW?"

"Always in a hurry, James; always in a hurry," he said, shaking his head. "Actually, the meaning of life is very simple."

I gave him a piercing look.

"Maybe another time," Jonathan said, shrugging his shoulders . He continued, "Okay, back to the question at hand; why are you here right now. Well my boy, and just so you know, after this I'm not going to let you cheat anymore. But in a nutshell, your life is at a standstill and you don't have the foggiest clue as to which direction to turn. Get it? FOGGIEST?? Ah, never mind," he said with a dismissive motion. "You're searching for something that is missing in your life and you're even lost in your quest to find it." Jonathan paused and smiled, adding, "See how this all works? How am I doing so far?"

"And you know all this, how?"

"Gee, let's see; you're afloat in an abyss without any sense of direction. You can't even tell if you're right-side-up or upside-down and yet you've got your fancy paddle in hand for when you make your decision to move forward. Hmmm, what could this possibly be telling you? Now let me think...," he said sarcastically. "What does that say to you, James? It's not rocket science. Any fool can come up with a complicated solution. It takes true genius to make it simple. $E=mc^2$; now that is simple. Don't make it more complicated than it needs to be. Complexity is an illusion. The best answers are always there in front of us to see, we just need to be tuned into them."

"Is that what you meant last night when you said, *'the secret is that everyone knows'*?"

Jonathan pointed his index finger at me like he was pointing a gun and said, "BINGO! There is a level where all is known and all we have to do is *listen* for it."

At that point Jonathan's canoe drifted a few feet away from my boat and I extended my paddle to him, thinking he'd grab it and pull our boats back together, but instead Jonathan just stepped out of his boat, took a step on the water and sat on the inflated edge of my raft.

74

"Great trick... how did you do that?" I said in amazement.

"What? Oh, that... Yeah, sometimes it works!" Jonathan said with a *green* twinkle in his eye. "Who ever said this abyss had to be wet and watery?"

"But we're in boats and I could feel us floating. Come on, you paddled over here."

"Ah, this is another example where you are clinging to what you expect," was all he said.

They sat in thoughtful silence. Jonathan pulled his right knee up to his chest, interlocked his fingers around his ankle and rested his chin on the top of his knee. He cocked his head in Jim's direction, still resting it on his knee and said, "Once again James, don't make things more complicated than they need to be. Dreams are where we learn that impossibility becomes commonplace. Dreams are also where we begin to understand that everything is possible...Even hooking up with that strawberry blonde you dream about."

I sat there quietly processing what Jonathan had said. I wondered if everything really could be possible.

"Now you're getting it," Jonathan said as if reading my mind.

I gave him a questioning look, because I hadn't said a word.

"I'm just finishing your thought," Jonathan said, shrugging his shoulders.

"It seems so easy in principle," I said, "but it only goes so far in the real world."

"Yes, but what is the real world, James? It's nothing more than our collective perception of what is real and what is not. Get enough people to believe in something and it becomes real."

"But...."

"But nothing," Jonathan said. "Science follows science fiction. Harnessing nuclear power and building the atomic bomb was just a theory until enough brilliant minds were brought together who believed it was possible. Their *faith* in their vision is what got it done. The same holds true with everything that has been created. Before anything can be brought into this consciousness, this existence, someone has to tap their imagination and believe that it can be. Belief is merely knowing that it *can* be done...Faith is knowing that it *will* be done. Some people find that too surprising but it just makes sense. It takes a dreamer to come up with what is thought to be impossible, but only those who *believe* can manifest that dream into existence. Hoping and wishing are wonderful things, but it takes *faith* to bring a dream into our reality. The word 'miracle' doesn't exist on the spiritual level. On that level *ALL* is possible and therefore nothing can be miraculous."

"So you are saying I need to believe...to have faith?"

"Well, that's where it starts. And trust me, *belief* can be very contagious, my boy."

"With that said, Jonathan walked back to his canoe and paddled away without another word. I just sat there in my raft and watched him fade away."

Jim got up from his chair with a grunt, checked on the steaks and said, "These hunks of cow flesh are ready. Grab a plate."

Chapter 7
The Pilot

Jim and Rabina filled their plates and sat at the round glass patio table. The conversation continued as they mowed down on their steaks.

"You mentioned your flight instructor before. What was her name; Josie?" Rabina asked.

Jim nodded as he shoved another piece of steak in his mouth.

"What's the story with her?"

Jim swallowed. "How do I begin to explain Josie?" he asked aloud. "Well, she's a real character. Let me preface this story by saying that when I met her, I was terrified of flying. I mean terrified!! I was white-knuckled every time I got in the plane to go skydiving, but I never let anyone know." Jim paused and pointed at Rabina, "And if you tell anyone, I'll deny it!" He continued, "I've been told that I'm a control freak; but the way I see it, when my life is hanging in the balance I want as much input and control as I can possibly have. I had thought about taking some flying lessons in the past, just so I knew what the plane was doing while I was in it. You know... I thought it would be a good thing to know if the plane was out of control and if I should be scared or not. But anyway, I just never found the extra cash to do it."

"You're afraid to fly?"

"Once again let me emphasize, if you tell anyone, I'll deny it!" he said with a grin. "Actually, I'm afraid of heights and I'm also claustrophobic, so being trapped in an airplane really isn't an ideal situation for me. It makes me feel completely helpless. And no one at the drop zone ever needs to know these little facts, okay?"

Rabina nodded with a devilish grin, as she knew she now had something on him. "Uh-oh, I sense another long story is on its way. I need more wine," she said with a chuckle.

Jim smiled back, "I get it... now I realize that you'll use any excuse for more alcohol. And for your information, my stories are only as long as they need to be. As I was about to say, *Fate*, the *Powers That Be,* call it whatever you want, has a way of stepping in and giving me a nudge from time to time when I need coaxing; or a good solid push when I drag my feet for too long. It took one of those *solid pushes* to make me a pilot. I swear it was as if *They* grabbed me by the shirt collar and pulled me to my fate." Jim paused, smiling directly at Rabina and said, "This is where Josie comes in. *The Powers* decided to have *Its* way with me, and led me to Josie's doorstep by a most unlikely path. I met Josie because of Kelly."

"Kelly? Kelly Neeker? From the drop zone?"

"Yep."

"She introduced you to Josie?"

"Yep again, well kinda..."

"Don't get me going on that girl; she just ain't right...she's made of broken glass and spiders."

"Well, would it help if I told you she introduced me indirectly? It began innocently enough one Sunday at the drop zone when Kelly was being particularly friendly."

Rabina interrupted, "I see where this is going already. What did SHE want? We all know that if she is showering you with compliments she's buttering you up for some kind of favor. Am I right? I am, aren't I? I knew it! She's so transparent."

"Don't hold back. Tell me what you *really* think of her," Jim said with a chuckle. "And you are so right; she waited until I was ready to leave that afternoon before she decided to pounce. She nonchalantly strolled over to my truck with an armful of books and flashed me one of her patented smiles."

"Let me guess; showing off her dimples?"

"But of course. She set the books on the open window ledge of the passenger door, poked her head into the cab over the stack of books and asked, "Would you mind doing me a big favor? I borrowed these books from someone, like a century ago, and I was wondering if you would do me a favor and drop them off for me."

"You mean she actually came right out and asked you directly for the favor?"

"Oh, let me finish...it gets better," Jim said, nodding. She said, "I thought I lost them in one of my moves but I found them on a shelf in my basement. They were in a box labeled 'kitchen stuff'. Can you imagine that? Could you please drop them off for me? It's kinda on your way home. Please? I promise I will call the woman and tell her you are stopping by with them before you get there. Please, please, please?"

"She came right out and asked you for a favor?" Rabina asked again, still amazed by that fact. "Wow, that's a new one... She's the queen of the subtle hint and a pro at using that 'uncomfortable silence' thing she does so well, but she actually came right out and asked...wow!"

"Yeah, I was just as surprised that she was giving the books back. Kelly has NEVER returned anything that has found its way to *her basement shelf.*"

"She must have needed the shelf space for something else she *borrowed.*"

"My thoughts exactly!"

Rabina added, "You know, Kelly could have a lot going for herself. She just refuses to grow out of her adolescent behaviors. She lives for the limelight and refuses to give up *Center Stage* to anyone. I think that's why she kinda floats on the fringe of the activities at the drop zone and never really fits in with the rest of the gang - except for Barney, and he's only receptive to her when there aren't any other eligible women around."

"Anyway, to make a long story a little shorter, I couldn't think of an excuse quick enough."

"So you did it for her? You gotta be kidding me!"

"What could I say? Kelly tossed a piece of paper with directions to Josie's house on the seat along with the books, said 'thanks' and disappeared before I could say anything. I drove off with a seat full of books and directions scribbled on the back of an envelope. She had written the directions using North-South orientation because she didn't know the names of any of the roads."

"Figures," Rabina added.

Jim continued, "I hate directions like that. You might as well say, "Go down this road and by some miracle of God, you will find the place." Needless to say, I zigged somewhere that I should have zagged and I ended up right where I knew I would end up - *lost*! I drove around for a while and was just about to give up when by a quirk of fate and that thing about *some miracle of God*, I came across Josie's place. It was just about dark when I found the name *The Gabriels* hand painted in black letters on the side of a dull galvanized mailbox.

It was a neat old house. The driveway leading to the house was just two ruts detoured around an old oak tree. It was probably a sapling when the house was first built. The house itself was an old country style, cedar-shake farmhouse with peeling white paint. The kitchen porch roof was sagging from age and neglect but still, it was a great place.

I pulled in the driveway, drove around that big old oak tree and parked near the house. I swear I could smell an apple pie cooling on the kitchen windowsill. Norman Rockwell would have been inspired to paint a scene using this place. As I got out of my truck and walked to the porch door with the books in hand, I wondered if Kelly had actually called ahead like she promised. I wasn't holding my breath about it."

"I'll lay odds she didn't," Rabina added.

"You'd win," Jim said with a grin.

"Can we try the *visual* stuff again? I'd rather *see* what happened next if you don't mind."

"Let's give it a try, but why don't we move inside before the mosquitoes eat us alive out here."

The two picked up their drinks and empty plates and moved into the house. After dropping the dirty dishes in the sink and topping off their glasses once more, they headed into to the living room. The *scene* started almost before they could get comfortable on the couch.

The windows and doors of the farm house were wide open and lit from inside, giving the place an airy feeling. Only the aluminum screens stood between the cozy interior and the cooling air of early evening. The air was filled with the smell of freshly baked something and the soothing rhythms of Japanese teiko drum music coming from somewhere in the house. It all fit; the house, the surroundings, the smells, the music. It was all so grounded and comfortable.

Jim glanced in the windows but didn't see anyone as he stepped onto the porch. He put his nose against the screen mesh of the kitchen door and cupped his free hand over the top of his eyes to help him see better as he looked into the kitchen for some signs of life. He was just about to knock on the wooden door frame when he felt something brush by his ear. He instinctively moved to swat it away, thinking it was a mosquito from the first hatching of the year. He was more than a little surprised to catch a handful of someone's index finger. He made an audible *girlish* sound as he dropped the books.

He dropped his shoulder and snapped his head around to find a woman in her early sixties with a huge smile and a surprised expression on her face. She pulled her finger from his hand and placed her hand on her hip saying, "Hey kiddo, I thought you heard me come up behind you. Sorry, I didn't mean to startle you. You might wanna get your hearing checked." Then she added, "And you really need to learn to relax some or you'll have a heart attack…you going to be all right?"

Jim stumbled for words, but before he could say anything, she asked, "What can I do you for?"

He composed himself just enough to stammer something about how he was making the book drop for Kelly. "I was just dropping off some books for Kelly…didn't she call to tell you I was coming?"

"Kelly?" she said with a surprised chuckle, "You didn't really think she'd actually take responsibility for her actions, now did you?" Glancing at the books, she added, "To be honest, I didn't think I'd ever see them again. If you know Kelly at all, you'd know that once she *borrows* something, that's the last time you'll you probably ever see it."

"So why would you lend them to her then?" Jim asked.

"Well, I believe that when I give someone a book to read, I don't really expect to get it back, especially from the likes of Kelly. I figure if the book means that much to them, they can have it. If a book does somehow make its way back to me, I believe that I'd better read it again because there's something else in it that I need to learn. It looks like I've got a lot of re-reading to do," she said, in a tone that left Jim believing that she had every intention to read each of the books again. She paused and then said, "Come on inside, I've got bread that's ready to come out of the oven. I'll put a pot of coffee on."

Jim had barely gotten the books picked up from the deck when he found himself sitting at the kitchen table and she was pouring him a big cup of coffee.

Jim found Josie to be a character right out of a Kurt Vonnegut novel. She somehow seemed bigger than life. She stood roughly five foot-seven, a little over weight and out of shape. Although her gray hair and pale wrinkled skin were signs that age and gravity had taken their toll on her physically, her eyes gleamed with the mischievous spirit of a child when she looked over the top of her glasses as she spoke.

Jim felt an instant rapport with this genuinely warm and caring woman. He drank coffee from a gray stoneware cup and ate a piece of homemade bread Josie had pulled hot and fresh from the oven and then lathered with real butter. There was nothing better! Jim's original plan was to drop off the books and head straight home but he was enjoying the impromptu visit and didn't feel any need to rush off. He was comfortable in his surroundings and found Josie's eccentricities quite charming. It was one of the few times Jim felt like he was right where he needed to be. He had forgotten about time; it just didn't seem to exist at the moment.

It was completely dark outside as Josie continued to pour an endless supply of coffee. "I didn't think to ask; would you like a little wine in your coffee?" Josie asked.

"I haven't done that since my grandfather passed away," Jim replied as he nodded his approval.

Josie disappeared momentarily into the pantry and re-appeared with a bottle. "Made it myself. I used to help my father when I was a young girl and I've continued the tradition after he passed away." Josie's face seemed to glow as she lost herself in memories of a joyful time with her father. "Every summer a truck would deliver cases and cases of grapes right to our cellar doors and I'd help Pa carry the crates down the steps. You know, I'm not even sure where he bought them…anyway, they'd just show up and we'd start makin' wine." Her face returned to the present and said, "I feel close to him when I'm making a batch. It's as if he's looking over my shoulder as I'm mixing the ingredients, making sure I'm doing it right. I can hear him say, *'not too much sugar now. We don't want it too sweet'*."

She grabbed a small glass from the cupboard, held it up to the light and then wiped it against her blouse. She poured a splash of the wine into the glass and handed it to Jim for him to taste as if she were a wine steward. He put the glass to his lips and took a sip, expecting it to taste vinegary, as most homemade wines do, but to his surprise it was actually very good. He finished what was in the glass and looked at her and said, "This is good stuff, almost a shame to waste it by putting it in coffee."

She smiled contently and said, "I'm glad you like it, and there's plenty more in the pantry. Remind me later and I'll make sure a bottle goes home with you tonight when you leave." She held the bottle in the air in front of Jim's cup, silently waiting for his approval to pour some in. He nodded, and she poured until it was near the brim of the cup and then set the bottle on the table between them as she sat down.

Their conversation had begun with talk about Kelly and the books he had returned for her. Talk then turned to the planting of asparagus and other general chitchat. As the night progressed, the coffee was substituted with more wine and the topics of conversation changed to astronomy, life on other planets, karma, reincarnation, and eventually airplanes and flying. Once the subject of flying entered into their conversation Josie stood and walked toward the kitchen window, grabbed an old gray flashlight from the window sill and motioned for Jim to follow her. She led him out to a large garden area somewhere in the darkness. She moved the light beam from left to right and back again as she explained where she would be planting her asparagus this season.

As they walked around in what would become rows of sprouts by summer, she began telling him that she had been a flight instructor since nineteen forty-six, right after World War II ended.

"I became a pilot long before it was fashionable for a woman to be anything other than a secretary or nurse," she said. "I learned to fly in a patriotic effort to help the War Effort during World War II. The 'birds,' as we girls called the planes, were being built in the factories here in the states and needed to get to the boys in the European theater. There weren't enough strapping young men to ferry the new airplanes to England, so the government taught some of us girls how to fly them. That all happened toward the very end of the war. Those were some great times," she said, lost in her thoughts. "And I've been flying ever since…I can't imagine having done anything else in my life. I still have a little Cessna that I keep out at Carter airport, just a stones' throw from where you kids skydive. For the most part, I'm pretty much retired but I feel the need to take on a student or two every once in a while. Teaching students keeps me on my toes and it helps keep the blood flowing to this old brain of mine."

Jim listened intently to her stories and made no attempt to ask why she had taken him out here into the chilly night air. Without any indication of forethought, she turned and headed back in the direction of the house. Jim followed. As they were walking out of the garden, Josie turned in what seemed like mid-stride and shined the flashlight directly in his face. The beam of light blinded him but he could imagine her looking over the top of her reading glasses at him as she said, "So when do you want to start? Don't worry, we'll take care of that fear you have of flying. That accident you had …well, that was in the past. We only need to worry about right now, and right now we're going to teach you to fly and get you past all that fear. Fear is a dreadful thing; it paralyzes a person. It stops you from enjoying life and doing the things you need to do."

Her offer came out of thin air and his first thoughts were, 'What accident, and why me?' Jim hadn't expressed any interest in flying. But what confounded him more than anything was that she knew he had a fear of flying. He began to speak, "How did you know… why… ah… ah… let me start over. I jump out of airplanes for cry'n-out-loud, so how would you know I have a fear of flying, and why would you want to teach me to fly? What makes you think that I want to learn to fly anyway?"

"Why this, why that; why, why, why," she said, shaking her head from side to side as Jim's eyes began to adjust to the light.

"Sometimes you ask too many questions." She looked at him as if she was expecting him to confirm her observation. He just shrugged his shoulders. She smiled, turned as if on cue, and continued walking toward the house with the beam of the flashlight bouncing through the darkness.

Jim, once again blinded by the darkness, followed behind her as best he could, like a little puppy dog chasing after the dimming light. As he walked, he rationalized that Kelly could have told Josie about his fear of flying and together they had concocted this plan just to get a rise out of him. It would have all made sense if it wasn't for the fact that he had never told anyone about his fear of heights, especially Kelly, so she had no clue of his aversion to flying. Besides, it didn't sound like Kelly and Josie were very close, so that idea was a bit farfetched.

When they got back to the warmth of the kitchen, Jim sat down again at the table and poured a little more wine into his cup while Josie busied herself, preparing a small plate of cheese, grapes and crackers. He waited for her to say something about the comments she made outside but she seemed preoccupied with her snack preparation. His curiosity finally got the best of him. "I gotta ask…how did you know that I have a fear of flying?"

She smiled at him, but this time with a somewhat perplexed look on her face. "Just one of my gut feelings, I guess. I began having these *feelings* as a young girl, right after my grandfather passed. Well, I actually get more than just a feeling; it's more like I'm watching a television show about the person's life. I get it all…the sights, the sounds and sometimes I even get the smells that go along with it. It's actually better than TV, now that I think about it. It's as if I'm watching the whole experience from a reclining chair at the edge of the stage. These *episodes*, as I call them, have gotten even stronger since my father passed away, god rest his soul. I see what drives a person and what's holding them back."

"So what do you see that drives me?"

"Knowledge," she said without hesitation, and then she added, "Well, knowledge and curiosity. You are one of those people who believes there's more to life than a nine-to-five job and a house with the white picket fence. You're driven to know more."

"Yeah, I'd like to think you're right about that." Jim took time to let what was said sink in and then asked, "Okay then, what do you see that's holding me back?"

"Well, Jim, in general, I see things that have traumatized a person's life...both in their current life and also in their past time-lines," she said matter-of-factly and then shrugged adding, "I never questioned the gift." She summed up her experiences by saying, "If it ain't broke, don't fix it."

"Past time lines...are you talking about past lives?" he asked.

She just shrugged her shoulders again. "Call it what you want."

"And what about this accident you talked about?" Jim asked.

She gave him a motherly look and said, "We'll talk about your past lives in due time, but not tonight," and she dropped the subject. Jim's natural curiosity wanted to push Josie for more answers about this *accident* but he knew that he wouldn't get any satisfactory answers until she was ready to talk. There was no point in pushing the issue; she would explain only when she was good and ready.

He had been involved in a couple of minor fender benders over the years but he was sure by the way Josie had mentioned something about *past lives*, she was referring to an *accident* that she felt had happened a lifetime ago. He didn't really believe in past lives and couldn't understand how an accident, now or in one of those past-life things, could explain his fear of flying.

The conversation turned to the subject of her 'gut feelings' and how she thought he could conquer his fear by learning to fly. He tried again to find out more about his *accident* but she just patted his hand and said, "Be patient, we'll talk about that when you are ready."

"Ready for what?"

"Are you a five year old waiting for Santa to show? Be patient, Jim, be patient. Everything in its own time."

He knew she wasn't going to expand anymore on the subject so he changed gears and asked why she was willing to take the time to teach him to fly. She replied, "It's what we are supposed to do."

"Who's this *WE* you talk about? Is there an invisible someone here who's going to help you?"

"No...I'm talking about me and YOU; that's the 'WE' I'm talkin' about. Teaching should never be a one-sided thing. It's got to be a win/win opportunity where everyone gets something positive out of the experience. I have no doubt that we will both benefit from it; besides, as I said, it keeps my mind young. But what it does for the rest of the body remains suspect." she said with a chuckle. "Now to answer your question about invisible people helping me; I don't actually see or hear anyone, but I do feel that I get guidance from a voice somewhere inside myself. I think we all do, if we are willing to listen to it." She looked at him, again shrugging her shoulders and said, "You will learn to listen more to that voice as well, but right now it's time for you to go. I'm tired and I want to do a little reading before I go to sleep." As they got up from the table, she raised her index finger into the air, shaking it as if she had just remembered something. Without a word she disappeared into her pantry and reappeared with a textbook and a bottle of wine. She placed the book in his hand and tucked the bottle of wine under his arm.

"This book is a good place to start studying for your ground school test, and the wine... well, it's just good anytime." She walked him to the door and turned on the outside light. "Have a safe ride home, and we'll talk sometime later this week."

As he drove away, the kitchen lights went out and the *scene* switched to Josie and Jim sitting shoulder to shoulder in a tiny two-seat airplane on the tarmac at the end of a runway.

Rabina asked, "What's going on now?"

Jim, with his eyes still closed, responded, "I'm not positive, but I'm in the left seat and by that anxious expression on my face I think it's my first flying lesson."

"Why are we seeing this?" she inquired.

"Your guess is as good as mine. You want to keep watching?"

"Oh, yeah! I was just wondering what it was all about."

"Well, I think we're going to find that out shortly."

Josie pushed a button on the left side of the steering yoke and spoke into the microphone attached to her headset. Jim heard her voice in his headset as she said something about departing runway two-three.

"Who are you talking to?" he inquired. "There's no control tower around here, is there?"

She patted his leg and smiled saying in a motherly tone, "Just making an announcement to anyone who can hear us, dear. It's just like praying... we broadcast our intentions and let the *Powers-that-Be* know where we are and what we're intending to do. Are you ready to go?"

Jim took a deep breath and nodded as Josie pushed the throttle knob on the instrument panel all the way forward. The engine revved to twenty-five hundred rpm's. Jim swallowed hard as the airplane began moving forward. They accelerated down the runway until Josie pulled back gently on the yoke with just a couple of fingers. The plane nosed up slightly and eased off the ground, beginning its climb. Once she had gotten the plane up to three thousand feet, she leveled off and pulled back on the throttle slightly, dropping the revs to twenty-one hundred. She pushed the nose down a bit and turned the trim wheel located between the seats until they were flying level.

"Ok, she's all yours," Josie said as she let go of the yoke and set her hands relaxed in her lap. With the plane trimmed in level flight and her sitting next to him in that cramped cockpit, there wasn't much he could do to cause much trouble, but he still didn't feel safe. As he put his feet on the rudder pedals and grabbed the yoke with his left hand, he had a sinking feeling that whatever he did would be wrong and he'd send them plummeting back to the ground with the plop of a giant cow pie. Josie first had him make a shallow turn to the left and then to the right, using both the yoke and the rudder pedals to perform what's called a coordinated turn.

"OK, now do the same thing, but I'm going to add full power," she said. She pushed the throttle knob all the way forward. Jim pushed the yoke slightly forward and nervously continued making the turns she requested until she pulled the knob back to the cruise position. He eased off the forward pressure on the yoke.

She slapped him lightly on the leg and said, "See what you're doing?"

"Ah… trying to stay alive?" he said, not having a clue what she was referring to. "Am I doing something wrong?"

"Quite the contrary…you're doing everything *right*. You've obviously done this before. I knew from the moment you showed up on my kitchen porch that you had been a fly-boy."

For the first time Jim stopped staring out of the front window and looked at Josie. "What? I've never flown before."

"Sure you have. Look at the way you hold the yoke."

"What do you mean?"

"You hold it with only three fingers; students never do that. If you were as green and afraid of flying as you claim, you'd have a death grip on that thing. And your turns, they're perfectly coordinated. You used just the right amount of rudder. Even under power you held altitude and used more right rudder to hold your heading. That is not something a first time student would know anything about. You were definitely a pilot…probably during World War II… Navy boy, I'm guessing; English, I believe."

"*Were*? … past tense? Are you talking about that past-life stuff again?" Jim asked skeptically, and then added, "Believe me, I've never flown a plane before."

"Maybe you haven't in this lifetime. Trust me, Jimmers, I'm never wrong about these things."

"And I'm supposed to believe that I was a pilot because you say so?"

With that said, Josie took the controls and pulled the yoke full back toward her chest, pitching the airplane sharply upward. She held it like that until the plane began to shudder. An alarm sounded loudly, announcing that the airplane was about to stall. When it did finally stall, the nose dropped toward the ground as the craft snapped violently to the right and began to spin in ever tightening circles.

"What the hell are you doing?" Jim shouted, confusion and fear gripping him hard. He pushed the yoke forward to the neutral position as he kicked hard left rudder. The plane rolled a couple more times to the right before it stopped spinning. When the plane regained airspeed, Jim pulled back on the yoke, taking the plane out of the dive and back to level flight. Nearly speechless, he looked at Josie and said, "What the hell!?"

Josie sat relaxed in her seat, her hands still in her lap and a content smile on her face. "Never flew a plane before, huh?" she asked. "So if you've never flown before, how do you explain knowing how to not only pull the plane out of a stall, but a stall *and* a spin? You didn't hesitate. You did exactly what you knew had to be done."

Jim was silent for a moment and then said, "I've had enough for today. Can we go back now?"

"If that's what you want to do...but it's not going to change the fact that you know how to fly. Get used to it."

"If that is true, why do I have such a fear of flying?"

"I think the answer is to be found somewhere within your recurring dream."

"What dream?"

"The one where you wake up in that quaint farmhouse somewhere in the French countryside with your head all bandaged up and the bad guys kicking in the door."

Jim looked at Josie in amazement. "How do you know about that dream?" he asked.

"I told you...I have that gift...I see things. Besides, I don't think it's a dream. I think it's a memory from your last life." Josie continued, "I know it's a lot to deal with, but it's part of why you're afraid of flying."

"Can we talk about this on the ground?"

"If you wish, but I think you need to talk about it now. What if I fly and you talk?"

"Only if you promise not to put us into any more stalls or anything like that again. I hate roller coaster rides!"

"I promise," she said as she took the yoke, glanced over the instruments and gave the trim wheel a slight turn. She then looked at Jim, smiled and said, "Okay, the plane is happy, so start talking, kiddo."

"I still can't believe you just did that. I could've had a heart attack."

"What are you talking about? I just trimmed the plane," she said, knowing that's not what he was referring to.

"Not that!! That stall thing you did."

"But you didn't have a heart attack, now did you? Ok, I can be a bit cynical at times but I had to prove to you that you do know how to fly."

"You couldn't think of another way?"

"It was the quickest way... and it worked, didn't it? Now tell me what you know."

"The dream seems to always begin as the aftermath of some big event of some kind."

"What makes you say that?"

"Well, it always starts out with this guy lying in bed with his head bandaged and arm in a sling. I'm pretty sure it's me and I'm in my early to mid-twenties. Even though it's a dream, there's a feeling that something significant had happened leading up to that scene." Jim paused, thinking, "There's not much more to the dream, really... There I am, lying in bed recuperating from the head injury and other bumps and bruises, when all of a sudden I hear gunfire outside. Before I can get out of bed to see what's going on, these guys in dark uniforms and big boots kick in the door. Then I wake up in a cold sweat and realize that it's a bad dream and I can't get back to sleep. The end."

"When did you start having this memory?"

"I've had it for as long as I can remember. Why do you ask?"

"That's why I'm thinkin' that it's more than a dream...and probably a past memory. You *were* a pilot during World War II."

"Yeah, you already said that. You also said that you think I was English. Is that why I like to sprinkle vinegar on my fish and chips?" he said with a grin.

"Probably," She said lightly, as if it could really be the reason.

"If you know what happened to me, will you fill me in on the rest of this story? It would be nice to put an end to those dreams, Jim said.

I wish I could help you, but unfortunately I don't know the whole story...I just get small pieces here and there. What I can tell you is your dream is a memory from your last life and it involves an airplane accident... hence your fear of flying. I think you crashed but managed to somehow walk away from it, and that's how you ended up at that farmhouse."

"What does it all mean?"

"I can't help you there either, but I have a feeling that it's all tied to you needing to remember you have been a pilot."

The scene faded, and Jim and Rabina found themselves once again looking at each other. Jim reached for his glass of wine and took a big drink. There was a prolonged silence; Rabina was first to speak. "Did it all happen like that?"

"Yeah, it was a frickin' rerun except this time I got to watch it all as a spectator. I surprised myself at how well I recovered the plane from that stall...pretty cool! God, how I hate stalls!"

"Did you ever find out if it was a memory or just a dream?"

"Nah, not yet."

"Have you had that dream again?"

"Yup... a couple of times. Same dream; it begins the same and ends the same, but I think I know how it turned out."

"Speaking of dreams...has today been one big dream, or did all this really happen today? I mean, we've experienced some really weird stuff." Rabina said.

"This is what I've been trying to tell you... I've been experiencing this kind of stuff for months now...except for the *dying thing*...that, of course, was a first," Jim said, tongue in cheek.

Rabina took a deep breath, "I'm exhausted...would you mind taking me home?"

"You're welcome to crash here," Jim offered.

"Very funny."

"What? You know I've got a guest room ready to go."

"Do you realize what you just said? *Crash here?* "

Jim shrugged his shoulders, "Sorry, poor choice of words. Let me rephrase that; you're welcome to *sleep* here. I just cleaned all my junk off of the bed in the guestroom. It even has clean sheets...and that doesn't happen very often," he said with a chuckle.

"Thanks, but I'd feel better waking up in my own bed tomorrow morning...very, very late tomorrow morning!"

"Yeah, I know what you mean. Come on, I'll take you home."

The two were silent on the way to Rabina's apartment, lost in their thoughts. They were only blocks away from her place, when Rabina suddenly said, "Oh my gosh... I know!"

"You know what?" Jim asked.

"I know what happened when the Nazi's showed up!"

"What Nazi's?"

"Those guys...in your dream...the ones in the black uniforms. The guys who knocked down the door were Nazi's. *Those guys were Nazis*! Gestapo or something!!"

"How do you know this?"

"I don't know how I know...it just came to me, but it's all so clear, I know it's got to be true! Josie was right; you did have an accident... that is, if crashing an airplane qualifies as an accident."

"Yeah, I'm pretty sure that would qualify as an accident."

"You weren't forced to punch-out, but your plane was heavily damaged from enemy gunfire. You were trying to limp the plane back to your base but you just couldn't keep it in the air long enough. You had to ditch it in a field in the south of France. Your plane skidded into a rock pile. You managed to get yourself out of the plane before it went up in a fireball...just like in the movies. Could that explain why you hate stalls?"

"I'd say yeah, that could do it."

"So, do you want to know what happened next, or should I keep you hanging for a while?" Rabina said with a grin.

"I think I already know what happened next, but there still seems to be a piece missing. I've gotten a glimpse or two as to where I was, and I know there were other people there....innocent people. I think a part of me doesn't want to know more."

"Do you know that after they broke down the door, one of them shot you?"

"My dream always ended just before that, but I kinda figured it had a dramatic finish."

They were now in front of Rabina's apartment. Jim pulled to the curb and put his truck in park. Rabina met Jim in the middle of the seat and they gave each other a long hug.

"Do you want to sit and talk about it?" Rabina asked.

"Another time... I'm pretty talked out right now. Do you mind?"

"Not at all... Are you going to be okay?"

"Yeah, I'm fine... I was just going to ask you the same thing. We both have a lot to process, don't we? Get a good night's sleep and we'll talk more when we're not so exhausted. Thanks for filling in some of the blank spots."

"Sounds good. Take care of you," Rabina said as she got out of the truck. Jim waited until she disappeared into her apartment before he drove away.

Jim went straight home to the comfort of his own bed.

Chapter 8
The Gift

Jim woke before daylight, comforted by the fact that he was in his own bed. He was almost never awake this early and wondered what morning people did at this ungodly hour of the day besides watch infomercials on cable TV. Being more of a night owl, it was obvious to him they couldn't possibly be very productive without at least a couple cups of coffee to get them going. He decided just to lie in bed and enjoy the half-asleep state that he was in. He was completely relaxed and surprised he didn't seem to hurt anywhere after hitting the ground as he had yesterday. His whole body should have been bruised, broken and sore; statistically he shouldn't even be alive. It felt wonderful just to lie there for a while.

He finally stretched a little, comfortable in knowing he didn't have anywhere that he needed to be. He didn't even care to know what time it was. Eventually he started to move and worked his way out of bed. When curiosity got the best of him and he finally did look, his alarm clock read 5:30. It was way too early in the morning to call anyone, so he grabbed his spiral notebook and began writing down every detail that he could remember from yesterday. He continued to write until almost eight o'clock, when he was satisfied he had gotten most of the details from his latest experience down on paper. What he may have missed, he knew he could always add when they came to him.

He closed his notebook and went downstairs into the kitchen knowing he needed to make a fresh pot of coffee. On his way to the coffee maker he saw the light from the answering machine still blinking from last night. He thought he should listen to the messages and then give Rabina a call to see how she was doing. He started a pot of coffee and pressed the *play* button on the machine. With the exception of a call from his mother, all of the messages were from people who either knew he had been involved in yesterday's accident or were wondering if he knew who had been. He was surprised by how many people he knew and even more surprised at how many had heard about the accident already. News travels fast.

The call from his mother was the usual invitation to dinner on Sunday. It was a weekly ritual that always included the phrase, "And if there's a special girl that you would like to bring along, we've always got enough food." There was no mention of yesterday's accident and he was relieved that she was unaware of the incident. After he finished listening to the messages, he called Rabina but got her voice mail. She was probably either still in bed or had already gone out for coffee. Whatever the reason, she didn't answer the phone so he left her the standard message to call him when she got the chance.

In the quiet of the morning his thoughts turned to what Rabina had said about his dream, and those thoughts made him think about Josie. He wanted to tell her about yesterday's events and Rabina's insights into his recurring dream. After all, Josie was the one who told him the dream was really a memory from another time and not just a bad dream. Even now that he had most of the pieces to the dream, he still didn't know what any of it had to do with him learning to fly in this life. Maybe it didn't mean anything at all.

He tried calling Josie but there was no answer at her house either. She didn't like phones in general and refused to own a cell phone or an answering machine on principal. She preferred to talk to people face to face.

Jim figured that Josie was probably somewhere on her property, out of earshot of the ringing phone, or simply chose not to answer. She was most likely doing her thing in the garden.

Unlike Jim, Josie seemed to enjoy unexpected company and he was sure she wouldn't mind if he dropped in without calling first. He decided to take the chance and drive out to her place and find her. Even if she wasn't home, it was a good day to take a drive and sort things out in his head.

He drove out to Josie's with his mind racing with everything that had transpired over the last few months, especially what had happened the prior day. He wanted to talk to her about that and also about the reasons he learned to fly.

As he drove, his mind wandered and different things from yesterday began to eat away at him. He hoped Josie would be home. The closer Jim got to Josie's old farmhouse the more he felt the need to talk to her. He needed her to give him her perspective and insights on these thoughts swirling in his head. Maybe she could shed some light on what had been happening. More than anything, he needed her to tell him everything was going to be okay.

Emotions began welling up inside of him and yesterday's events triggered an overwhelming need to pull it all together into some kind of coherent picture. He was hoping she could help him do that. He needed to talk and knew she would let him do that and not think he was out of his mind. That alone would make the visit worthwhile.

Jim reached her driveway and turned in. As he drove around the oak tree, he noticed tiny buds on the tips of its branches were beginning to show themselves, giving it a light pea-green hue. He parked his truck and began walking toward her kitchen porch when he heard her voice call to him, echoing off of the house wall. The voice came from behind him. He turned and saw Josie sitting comfortably in an oversized weathered cedar chair at the back corner of her garden. She was cradling a cup of tea in her lap. Jim was relieved he didn't have to go searching for her. He walked over to where she was sitting and said, "I'm so glad that you are here."

"Take a load off and sit for a while. Would you like some tea?" When she got a good look at the expression on Jim's face she realized that this wasn't just a social call and that he needed to talk. "Come, sit; talk to me. Sit and tell me what's on your mind," as she patted the chair next to her with the palm of her hand.

Jim sat down next to her and began talking non-stop, unraveling the experiences that had unfolded over the last few days. Josie listened without interrupting. When he finished she sat quietly for a moment with a nearly blank expression. Jim had never known her to be at a loss for words and he had expected her to have some kind of immediate answer for him. When there was none, he looked at her and asked, "Well…what do you think? Are these the dreams of an overactive imagination or am I having a series of psychotic episodes here?"

A content grin came to her face as she answered, "Neither! What I think you are having what I call a *Personal Insight*." She turned and faced him directly with a look on her face of sheer delight. She took his hand and sandwiched it between hers as she shivered with excitement and added, "Isn't it wonderful?"

"Wonderful? I'm wondering if I'm losing my mind...so, I'm not sure I would call it wonderful," Jim said. "I bounced and died. I gotta tell you...It's scaring the hell out of me. "

"Of course you're scared or you wouldn't be here talking to me about it," she replied.

He nodded in agreement and then said, "But I'm really confused by it all. I don't know how much more of this I can handle. Can you please help me sort these things out?"

"Relax Jimmers, I'll do what I can, but first take a deep breath and know this is just what you've been waiting for."

He looked at her with such a perplexed look on his face that he could feel the ferule between his eyebrows, but he said nothing.

"Don't look so serious...you've been searching for that *something* missing in your life and now it looks as if it's making itself known to you. It's a gift; embrace it."

"Embrace it how?"

"Accept it, learn from it... and more importantly, share it," she said.

"Share it? Share what?"

"Share your experiences...share everything that you are learning."

"Can you back up a little, because I'm not sure what I'm learning."

"Ah, but you will. All the pieces are coming together for you and once they do, you won't be able to contain yourself. Trust me, you'll want to share everything that you have learned. It's in your nature."

"Share it with whom?"

"When you learned to fly, did you keep that knowledge to yourself? Hell no, you shared your experience with anyone willing to listen to your stories. They got a chance to live vicariously through your experiences. That is why you have been given this gift."

"Is that what Jonathan was talking about when he questioned what I really learned from flying?"

"Maybe; you'd have to ask him what he meant, but don't confuse your learning experience with sharing those experiences with others. One rarely has anything to do with the other." She paused in thought. "I take that back. We almost always receive gifts for sharing our experiences, but that's never the main lesson." Josie paused again as a smile of satisfaction came to her face. "Jimmers, I knew when you were sent to me that you had a special gift. It's only now that you are beginning to see that gift yourself. In the past, the Powers have given you a glimpse from time to time to keep you searching...and learning."

"I still don't understand this gift...and why now?"

"That's simple... you are finally ready and it's your time. Everything you have done has been in preparation for this moment."

"Time once again!" Jim said quietly, recalling Jonathan's words.

"What do you mean, *again*?"

"I don't know. It was something that Jonathan said to me the first time we talked...well, the first time we talked, in my dream."

"Tell me about it."

Jim gave Josie a Readers Digest condensed version of his first meeting with Jonathan in his dream and concluded by saying, "And Jonathan's last words to me that day were; *"It's time_once again."* Now every time I see him, something else is happening and I haven't had a chance to ask him what he meant by it. The strange thing is, he keeps asking me if I remember where I've met him before."

"Interesting. Do you remember?" she asked, looking at him intently.

"Nah, not yet, but he looks so familiar; it seems like I should," he said, shaking his head. "Do you have any insight into that for me?" Jim asked.

"I have my suspicions but that's all they are at this point and I'm going to keep them to myself until I'm given more insight. I

99

don't want to say anything until I'm sure. My feeling is you'll have to figure that out for yourself or get what you need from Jonathan."

"In that case, I want to hear more about how *special* I am," Jim said whimsically.

"We are all special, Jimmers and don't put words in my mouth. What I said was that you had a special gift. You truly do; *that* I know."

"And what is this special gift?"

"Name something that you've attempted that you haven't succeeded at."

"Relationships and marriage," Jim quickly responded without needing to think.

"Those don't count."

"Why not?"

"Why not?" she repeated. Her eyes roamed toward the sky as she searched for the best way to explain herself. Putting her thoughts in order, she finally said, "Where do I start? Well, it doesn't count on so many levels. To begin with, you've chosen all of your relationships as part of your life experience. It's your lesson plan, so don't go playing the victim here. On top of that, you tend to see peoples' true souls and forget that you're dealing with people who are working on their own list of life experiences."

Jim looked at her quizzically.

She raised an eyebrow and continued, knowing exactly what Jim was thinking. "Yes Jimmers, you see their heart; you see them as they could be. You see the soul that they came into this world with. But remember, you've chosen to date each and every one of those crazy gals for the experiences they invoked in you," she said with a glimmer in her eye. She continued, "And the good news is that each relationship and experience lasted only as long as you both needed it to last."

Jim interrupted with, "There are a few I wish I didn't need to have experienced, as you put it."

She just smiled and continued. "The Powers have a unique knack for coordinating lesson plans. Remember, you can't force someone to change and you certainly can't change unstable women with affection. The best you can do is dance with them." She paused as if listening to a silent voice and continued once again. "We better learn from every choice we make and everyone we meet; good and not-so-good. If not, we have to go through the experience and same lesson over and over until we do. We learn what is important and what makes sense to us. So, when you are confused by their actions, take a good long look and ask yourself why you have chosen that experience and what lesson is in it for you... there is always something that is to be learned. Even that last dysfunctional relationship you finally dug yourself out of."

"Are you talking about Melody?"

"Yup! That wench...and I tell you, I'm being overly kind when I call her that. I hate to see how she used you the way she did. I'll say it again: you can't rehabilitate an unstable woman with affection. It just doesn't work. I know you saw her for who she could be, not for who she was in this world. Somewhere in a parallel universe she may have been that nice, deserving person you wanted to make her out to be but that's not what she is in this one."

Josie continued, "I hope you've learned the lesson you need to learn in there because I'd hate to see you have to go through that again. She's a very troubled girl, but in her defense, she's got her own lessons to learn too. Unfortunately she's choosing to ignore them....too bad, she'll have to experience her drama all over again."

"Do you really think she's that unstable?" Jim asked.

Josie looked at Jim with a caring motherly look, "Yes, I do. I'm entitled to my opinion, just as you are entitled to yours. I'm only saying this to help. Please keep in mind there are only two reasons why someone will criticize you. One, they are sincere and truly want to help you based on their perspective and experience. Or Two, they have a need to make themselves feel better by belittling you or trying to control you. You're the one who has to decide which of the two it is. If they are trying to help, take what they say in advisement. If it is the second, they have serious problems; ignore their cruelty and move on. They have issues that need to be worked out and it's not your responsibility to help them."

Jim's thoughts went instantly to the vicious and condescending note he had received from the writing instructor he had in college. The note stated that Jim didn't have a good enough grasp of the English language to ever entertain the idea of writing and conveying his thoughts on paper. Jim had taken the class for fun, never aspiring to be a writer and that note had cut to the bone. It was mean, vindictive and uncalled for. Jim had often wondered why the instructor had been so cruel. The note made more sense now, as Jim realized that the instructor was truly a pathetic little man. The poor aging instructor was a tortured *wannabe* writer who never made it and was simply venting his frustrations.

Josie and Jim sat in a contemplative silence. The sun was warm on their skin and the air smelled sweet. Birdsong carried through the trees on a fresh, gentle breeze. The sounds and smells of spring were markedly heightened.

Jim broke the silence, "So what you are saying is, I have no control over what happens in my relationships and they are just part of my getting-to-know-myself experience?"

"No, what you've got to keep in mind is that you chose and created those relationships for what they had to offer you. It's actually a self-exam. Relationships amplify the things in our life that we need to examine in ourselves. They force us to face who we are and where we are going. It's not always easy to walk away from a bad relationship because of the emotional investment you've made, but if you don't leave, it can cripple you. If you don't make changes, the lessons may never be learned because of fear or despair. Or even worse, you will never allow yourself true love."

"So what you are saying is that I can't count on having a lasting relationship?"

"Again, don't be putting words in my mouth. What I'm saying is that you've chosen all of your past relationships for their lessons and experiences."

"Tough lessons," Jim said.

"Only when you don't learn from them."

"My relationships always seem to start out good but over time their true colors show through and that's when things fall apart."

"That's because you see their soul and that's all you choose to see in your potential mate, not what they are this time around. If you use what you've learned from your past relationships, the next ones will improve. For instance, your involvement with Melody; a couple of ex-husbands and a bunch of kids... you should have expected a bumpy road. But however, you chose it for the experience. "

"What was I supposed to learn from that?"

"You're the only one who can answer that question. Just don't limit your experiences, Jimmers. Sometimes you have to accept those possibilities before you can have the future you want."

"But sometimes I feel as if I've spent too much time on the 'never possible' ones."

"No, you spent just the amount of time you needed to bring you to this point."

"How did we get on this subject anyway?" Jim asked, trying to lighten the subject.

"I believe it was when you said that you were a loser when it came to love," she said with a smirk.

"Ah yes, I remember…unfortunately. But I didn't actually say that I was a loser."

"Yes, you did; you were just a little more diplomatic and used nicer words."

"Well, now you've managed to pile a dose of depression on top of my neurosis."

"Glad I could be of help. Do you feel better now?" she said cynically and then added, "Things will change for you soon…I know this. You will find true love when you use the experiences you have gained in the past. You will find her soon enough and there will be more to the relationship than you imagined…mark my words."

"Whenever my father said *'mark my words'*, it always happened."

"That's because he was a smart and intuitive man who tapped into what the universe knows."

"I hope you are right about meeting the right woman soon."

"Jimmers…I guarantee it! And you will teach each other so much. It will be the most fulfilling experience you will ever have in this life."

Jim didn't question her words because he knew she was right…he could feel it in his bones.

"You know, I've got a niece that you should meet," Josie said waving her index finger upright in the air as if suddenly remembering something. "She's a beautiful girl...inside and out. Bright too...she's a doctor. You'd like her. She's a few years younger than you but the two of you have a lot in common. I think you'd hit it off. You both straddle the analytical and spiritual worlds. You're both Old Souls. I don't know why I didn't think of introducing the two of you sooner. I've got some pictures of her in the house. I'll have to show them to you when we go inside."

"Yeah, that would be nice." Jim replied, passing it off as just a well-meaning gesture.

"Now Jimmers, back to my question. Name me something you've attempted and didn't succeed at." And then she added, "Besides relationships."

"Let me think. I can never seem to get my house cleaned up. It's always a mess."

"Once again, it doesn't count. It's not that you can't, you simply choose not to. It's not a priority for you. That's just a lack of discipline on your part, and don't blame that on your mother either!"

"I wasn't going to blame it on her."

"Well, you better not."

"Okay, okay, I confess; I always seem to accomplish what I set out to do, but anyone can do that."

"No they can't!" she said with conviction. "Look around. How many people do you know that have accomplished what you have?"

"There are a lot of people who have not only done as much as me, but have done a lot more."

"Of course there are other gifted people out there. I didn't say that you had a corner on that market. All I'm saying is that you are gifted. You are unique and so are your gifts...use them! Others may be able to do the things that you can do, but no one, *and this is the key...NO ONE can do it the WAY you do!*" She looked into his eyes to make sure that what she was saying was sinking in, not expecting a response. Jim looked at her and nodded. She smiled and nodded back, adding. "Now...are you ready for that cup of tea?"

"Sure," Jim said as he sat back in the chair.

"You know, I'd get it for you but I'm so comfortable I just don't want to move. Years ago I would have jumped right up and ruined this beautiful feeling just to get you a bloody cup of tea, but I've learned to savor these moments. So, if you want it, you're going to have to get it yourself," Josie said. "And as long as you're up, get me some too!" She extended her cup, adding, "It's one of the advantages of being old; I'm not expected to be everyone's servant anymore." She paused and then said, "Go...you know where the cups are. There's hot water on the stove and tea bags on the counter just to the right, in the little box."

Jim had a smile on his face as he walked into the kitchen and found the cup, water and tea bags right where Josie said they would be. He fixed himself some tea and then returned to the garden with her empty cup, a tea bag and enough hot water to refresh their cups once they were empty, as well. He once again took his place in the chair next to her. He still had the smile on his face.

"Why the smile?" Josie asked.

"I get a kick out of you."

"That is what my wasband used to say."

"Wasband? You mean your husband, John?"

"No, my ex-husband...hence the emphasis on *was*-band."

"You're so eccentric. I never have to guess what you're thinking. You just say whatever is on your mind."

"Eccentric... now that's not a term that I hear very often, but I'll take that as a compliment. Did you ever realize that that term is usually reserved for the quirky actions of the extremely rich? Everyone else is just considered *strange* or *weird* but the rich are entitled to be *eccentric*. Well, I'm not rich, but when you get to my age you do what you want instead of doing what everyone else thinks you should be doing. Life is too short to not be doing what you want to do."

"Wow, I got that same message from Jonathan yesterday after I bounced."

"Well, you must have needed to hear it again."

"Yeah, I guess so." Jim paused for a moment and then asked, "Josie, what am I supposed to do with all these bizarre experiences I've been having?"

"Write them down and share them," She answered without hesitation.

"I have been writing it all down."

"But that's not enough. You've got to share it. You need to publish your experiences for others to read."

"What do you mean by publish it, as in something like a book? I can't write a book. I don't know how to do that."

"Why not? You didn't know how to do the other things that you've done in your life when you set out to do them....Now did you?"

"Well, you've got a point there."

"Of course I do."

"I guess it comes down to the fact that there's always been this thought in the back of my head that I'm not ready or that I'm not old enough to do something."

"Haven't you been learning that nothing is impossible?"

"What could I possibly say that hasn't already been said?"

"Pick a noun..."

"What?"

"Pick a noun...any noun, Josie prompted emphatically

"Why?"

"Just pick *any* noun. There are lots of them...Tree, car, dog; pick one."

"Ok, car."

"Is there only one way to make a car?"

"No."

"There are a lot of different makes and models out there. There are so many different variations on the concept of a few wheels and a power source. Wouldn't you agree? Find *your* voice! Let me remind you once again; you are unique and no one can tell a story, *your story*, the way you will. The writer Anais Nin once said, *'The role of a writer is not to say what we all can say, but what we are unable to say'*."

"Think of your story as a loose thread, start pulling that thread and let it unravel."

"You say *will,* as if it is a sure thing. Josie, I barely passed creative writing 101. The instructor said that I didn't have a grasp of the English language, much less any talent for writing."

"Yes, he did say that, but don't you see? Your instructor behaved like a narrow-minded twit toward you for a reason. He had no other purpose in your life; he had no real talent as a writer himself or even as an instructor for that matter. You created him to challenge you and to prove him wrong. His only real purpose in your greater scheme of things was to test you...to see if you were going to believe what he told you or if you had more faith in your own abilities."

"How do you know that?"

"I've told you that I sometimes see things; that happens to be one of them. Now are you going to put pen to paper and write down what you know or are you going to do what your instructor expected of you?"

"What can I say? So many great books have been written in this genre. Just off the top of my head I can name *Way of the Peaceful Warrior, the Tao of Pooh* and *Carlos Castaneda's* whole series of books and nothing speaks better about this stuff than the little book by *Richard Bach* called *Illusions.*"

"Jimmers, write it from your heart...write it for yourself. Write it for those who need it. As they say, write it and they will come."

"That's 'Build it and they will come'."

"You know what I mean. You have found the books you have needed. Those people who need to find your words will as well...trust me." She looked straight into his eyes and added, "With only your words, you can move mountains."

"Move mountains, huh? With just my words?"

Josie nodded.

"Wow...but why would I want to do that? The mountains seem perfectly fine right where they are," Jim said to lighten the serious nature of the conversation.

"Joke all you want. Change the subject if you wish. Do nothing if that is what you choose to do, but you asked for my input and I'm giving it to you. I think you need to do this...for yourself if not for anyone else."

"I believe you, but how do I write it? What do I say that hasn't already been said?"

"Say it in your own way. Once again, no *one can say it the WAY you do!* Just pull on all those loose threads and it will write itself...Your own personal 'string theory', as it were. The only question is; when will you start?"

"Thanks a lot. That remark was so very Zen-like of you," Jim said sarcastically, and then asked, "Seriously Josie, where would I begin?"

"With a first step...pick a spot, Jimmers. You started your skydiving adventure by going to the drop zone and taking that first step out of the airplane." She paused, wanting to pick her words carefully so they would make the impact she wanted. "You're not intended to write the quintessential book on the 'Powers-that-Be.' Even if you could, no one would understand it anyway. You can only tell your story and let people take from it what they will."

"Well, you've definitely given me a lot to think about."

"Do more than think about it. It's important that you act."

"It sounds like you are trying to tell me what to do."

"No, I'm telling you what you are *intended* to do." She paused in thought and then added, "Jimmers; again, I really think you *need* to do this for yourself as much as for those that will read, and benefit from what you have to say."

"You sincerely believe that, don't you?"

"It's much more than a belief...it's a knowing. Now go home and write. You'll be surprised to see where it leads you. You need to do this to help make better sense of things. It will be a very cathartic experience for you." She paused and with a fanning motion of her hand, said, "Now go."

"I think I'll go now." He thanked her for listening, gave her a long hug and walked to his truck.

Chapter 9
The Visitor

Jim left Josie's place with an energy coursing through his body that he'd never felt before. She had reassured him that he was moving in the right direction and everything was okay, even though he wasn't sure of what direction he was going or what *everything* encompassed. He smiled to himself.

He had goose bumps on his arms, not from the mental stimulation he had gotten from the talk with Josie, but from the chill in the air as the sun was now slowly sliding toward the western horizon. He rolled up his windows and turned the heater on high.

On the drive home he realized his earlier anxieties were gone and he now had a slight buzz of euphoric possibilities. The music on the radio seemed to be playing just for him as he floated down the road. At one point he reached over and scribbled some thoughts into his opened notebook before they were overrun by new ideas. The one question that kept making its way to the forefront of his thoughts was…now what do I do with all this stuff I've been experiencing?

When Jim got home he put his truck in the garage and walked into the house. Once inside, he tossed his keys on the snack bar near the door. As he walked through the kitchen he realized that he had been so preoccupied all day that he had forgotten to grab something to eat. A couple cups of tea with honey at Josie's were all he'd had. He wondered what he might find as he opened the refrigerator door. There was a cardboard box containing the remains of a pizza on the top shelf; the leftovers from a couple of nights before. It would be enough to satisfy his hunger. He grabbed a slice of the cold Canadian bacon, green olive and mushroom pizza from the box and retrieved a cold beer from the crisper drawer. He balanced the box containing the rest of the pizza on the unopened can of beer and closed the fridge door. He set the box on the kitchen counter, knowing that he would finish the contents before he was done. He walked into the living room, pizza slice in hand, and turned on the TV. It became background noise as his mind pondered how he could tell his story. He wandered aimlessly through the house, pacing back and forth, roaming from room to room as if he was hoping to find the answer to his questions hidden in one of the corners of his home.

As the night progressed, the pizza disappeared along with several beers leaving only recyclable material. With his hunger satisfied, he stopped his pacing and melted into the couch. His body was in a near horizontal position, covered from his waist to his bare feet with a well-worn afghan his mother had lovingly made for him years ago. Somewhere in the middle of a program on the Discovery Channel, he heard a knock on his backdoor.

He had the same comfortable feeling that Josie described earlier, and he knew that he'd forfeit that wonderful feeling once he moved. He hesitated for a moment before making a move to get up. Jim could only hope to reclaim that feeling later, when he once again could return to the couch.

Jim reluctantly moved anyway and as expected, the magical 'good feeling' spell was broken. He shuffled barefoot into the kitchen toward the back door.

He turned on the outside light and glanced out of the window before he opened the door. As he peeked out the window, he didn't immediately see anyone. What he did see was a basket of nectarines sitting on the top step. A dozen fresh, ripe nectarines carefully placed on a red and white plaid cloth in a hand-crafted wicker basket. It looked like something right out of a photo shoot from Family Circle magazine.

He smiled to himself as his imagination ran wild with the mental image comparing the basket of fruit on the porch step with a piece of cheese in a mousetrap. He looked around but saw no one. If someone was there watching, they were hiding in the shadows. He opened the door, crouched down and plucked a small note card nestled neatly among the nectarines. He read the note in the yellowish glow of the outside bug light above his door. It was hand written in calligraphy and read: *An apple a day will keep the doctor away, but nectarines are sweets for the soul.* At the very bottom of the note were the words: *Thoughts, Words, Actions = Experience*!! The note wasn't signed.

Jim looked around one last time for any sign of the person who had delivered the basket, but there was none. As he turned back toward the door, he noticed a splash of color along the house. It was a tiny yellow rose in full bloom growing just a couple of feet from the door. He bent over it for closer examination. He knew he hadn't planted it and wondered how it had gotten there. Jim held his nose to the rose petals and took a deep breath. It definitely was alive and growing. This flower shouldn't be blooming this time of year, he thought. He pulled his Swiss Army knife from its case on his belt and cut the flower from the vine, carrying it into the house along with the basket of fruit.

Once inside, and in better light, he inspected the contents of the basket. Whoever left the nectarines either knew that they were his favorite or made a lucky guess. Nectarines were like peaches without the fuzz. The fuzzy skin on a peach gave him the willies just like the sound of fingernails on a blackboard does to others. He grabbed a nectarine from the basket and bit into it. It gushed with a juice so sweet and delicious that it surprised him. It made him stop and look at the nectarine with a new appreciation. He dug around in one of his upper cabinets near the sink and pulled out a glass milk bottle, filled it with water and dropped the rose in it. He returned to the living room and pushed the mail to the side - some opened, some not - and made room for his little splash of color.

He parked himself on the edge of the couch, keeping the basket of nectarines within easy reach on the coffee table. He had a second nectarine, now half eaten, in one hand and the note from the basket in the other. The Discovery Channel played in the background as he contemplated the words on the note; *Thoughts, Words, Actions = Experience.* He wondered if this somehow tied in with the other recent events or if it was pure coincidence? Did Rabina or Jonathan leave the basket as some sort of gag? Could he dare hope that his private Little Red Riding Hood be the strawberry blonde visitor from the drop zone? He wanted to imagine that it was she who left the basket on his step and that she was too shy to give the basket to him personally. He smiled to himself; he liked that scenario, but knew that it was a bit farfetched. Since there was no way of knowing who left the goodie basket, he went back to the significance of the note.

What was he supposed to *think*, *say* and *do* to give him the *experience*? He finished the second nectarine and sat back a little deeper into the couch, licking the juice off his fingers while contemplating having yet another nectarine. At the same time he wondered what would give him the answers he was looking for. He decided to call Rabina again to check on her and see if she had anything to do with this. He could also tell her about his visit with Josie. He picked up the phone and dialed Rabina's number. The phone rang endlessly in his ear but Rabina didn't answer. As he waited for her voice-mail to kick in, he glanced in wonder at the yellow rose sitting on the edge of his coffee table. There in the stack of mail next to the impromptu vase, sat a brochure with a little yellow rose in the corner of the page. He thought it odd and claimed it as an omen. He hung up the phone without leaving a message and pulled the sheet of thick glossy paper from the pile to look at it more closely. It was a three-color advertisement for a fabulous, once-in-a-lifetime opportunity to purchase his very own timeshare at the lovely Yellow Rose of Texas Condominiums. These were complete turnkey residences with two pools and a golf course in a gated community near sunny Galveston. Although he had owned a cowboy hat at one time and did enjoy Texas toast, that was the extent of his desire for things 'Texas'.

"Is this what I was supposed to read," he thought? Did the Powers-that-Be want him to own a timeshare in Texas? He smiled to himself and realized he was grasping at straws and could rationalize just about anything at the moment. He tossed the brochure back onto the stack of mail and decided to call it a night. He searched among the pillows and sofa cushion beside him for the TV remote, but couldn't find it. He eventually found it buried under the stack of mail on the table.

He was about to turn the TV off and call it a night, when he heard the narrator say, "*ARISTOTLE believed that courage allows us to define who we are rather than letting society or someone else determine that for us. With courage, we are the product of our own will. We sometimes create our defenses to protect ourselves from the anxiety of our choice of freedoms.*" Jim turned off the TV and chuckled, causing air to snort out of his nostrils. "Okay," he said to himself; "I've *thought* about it and now I'm speaking *words*...even if I am talking to myself. I'm going to take *action* ...I'm going to bed. Wow...What an *experience!* He was exhausted and headed for the comfort of his bed.

He went into the bathroom, brushed his teeth and then curled up in his bed with a Tom Clancy novel. He lost himself in the book and read until he couldn't keep his eyes open any longer. Rolling over, he turned off the reading light and began his slide into *La-La Land*. As he drifted, a thought came to him that must have been connected to what he had heard about Aristotle's belief in courage. Jim was almost asleep and yet he knew that if he waited until morning to write his thought down, it would get trampled by fresher thoughts and vanish forever. He turned the light back on and wrote: *"Fear, too often, makes us live our lives within the margins or boundaries that are allowed by others. If we can move beyond our fears, we move our boundaries...and those boundaries then become the new starting point."* With that written, he once again turned off the light and resumed his place amongst the sleeping.

Jim was in the middle of a dream involving a walk-bridge with a steep incline. He was having trouble walking up its soft, green trampoline-like nylon mesh without sliding backwards, when he heard a voice calling out his name. He woke up enough to realize that the *bridge* thing was a dream, but the voice he was hearing was real. There was someone outside his window calling out his name.

"Yooooo whoooo...Jimmyyyy. Are you awake?"

Jim wasn't the least bit surprised that he recognized the voice as Jonathan's. He got out of bed and followed the voice to his opened window and asked, "Jonathan, what the hell are you doing? Do you have any idea what time it is?"

"Let me guess...it's dark out so it must be sometime during the evening...right?"

"Why can't you ring a doorbell or knock like normal people?"

"I tried being normal once, but it just wasn't for me…way too boring," he said straight faced and then continued. "I'm glad that you're still awake."

"Well, YEAH…I am now! That tends to happen when someone outside my window is calling out my name. That has been known to wake a person up. What do you want?"

"I was hoping that you were in the mood for a beer."

"Jonathan…it's one o'clock in the morning," Jim said, annoyed. Jonathan stood silently looking up at the bedroom window like a three year old asking for a cookie. Jim looked at the clock again and decided that going out for a beer wasn't the worst thing. "Okay, I'll get dressed and be right down. Where do you want to go?"

"Well…actually, I was hoping we could just sit and have a few beers here."

"Alright, come on around to the front door and I'll let you in."

"I bet you've got some of that fancy imported stuff, don't ya?"

"Don't push it," Jim said with a smile.

Jim grabbed the pair of sweat pants that he had conveniently dropped on the floor when he got into bed earlier. He pulled a T-shirt over his head, went down the stairs and unlocked the front door, letting Jonathan in.

Jonathan smiled and nodded as he walked past Jim and headed directly toward the kitchen. Jim stood at the front door speechless, hand still on the doorknob. "Ah, come on in," he said after the fact. Jim heard the clattering of condiment bottles coming from the refrigerator. Jim shut the front door and walked into the kitchen to find Jonathan crouched down in front of the fridge, peering deep into the bowels of the lower shelf, searching for a beer. He looked up at Jim with a confused expression.

Jim smiled, "Can't find what you are looking for?"

"I thought you said that you had some beer in here," Jonathan said, puzzled as he craned his head to see into the far corners of the fridge.

Jim's smile widened. He stood silently, enjoying Jonathan's bewilderment. "I said I'd see what I had." He finally pointed toward the bottom of the refrigerator and said, "I think you'll find what you are looking for in the crisper drawer on the right, down there on the bottom. Just pull horizontally on that little handle there and beer will magically appear," he said with condescending humor.

Jonathan looked at Jim, cocking his head slightly to one side; "Crisper drawer, huh…what a concept!" He thought for a moment and then continued, "And why do *"we"* keep our beer in the crisper drawer?"

"*WE* keep it in the crisper drawer because *WE* want to keep it in the crisper drawer," Jim said firmly, astonished that it was one o'clock in the morning and he was defending his decision on where to keep his beer. Jim heard a voice in his head telling him to relax and enjoy the moment. The voice said, "If you were to die tomorrow, would this really matter?" He cursed the voice, then took a deep breath and exhaled. "It keeps the beer colder," Jim said, quickly explaining his logic.

"Ah!" Jonathan nodded, "That's why you get paid the big bucks." He opened the crisper and retrieved two bottles of Saint Pauli Girl Dark. He held one up and grinned at Jim. "Now that's what I'm talkin' about. I knew you'd have the good stuff…I just knew you would!"

He moved over to the kitchen table and sat near the window, placing both bottles of beer in front of him. He tried to twist the cap off of one of the bottles, but the cap wouldn't move. He made a second attempt, this time with a more concerted effort but the cap still didn't move. He looked at the bottle, somewhat puzzled. He set it down, grabbed the second bottle and gave that cap a twist. That cap on that bottle didn't move either. He held the bottle away at arms' length, inspecting it as if he was looking for some sort of secret lock.

Jonathan turned to Jim and made a hand gesture that was a cross between *confusion* and *help me, I'm thirsty.*

"They don't twist off," Jim said with a smile. He reached up for the bottle opener conveniently affixed to the side of the refrigerator by a magnet. He held the opener up in the air, "To open good imported beer, you're going to need this magical little device," he said, and he handed it to Jonathan.

"I'll make a note of that," Jonathan said as he grabbed the opener. He inspected it for a moment and then used it to remove the cap from the bottle. He looked up at Jim with a sheepishly content expression and with a hand motion offered Jim a seat at the table.

"Don't mind if I do," Jim said

Jonathan popped the cap off the second bottle of beer and slid it in front of Jim.

"So, back to my original question…what brings you here at this ungodly hour?" Jim asked.

"I told you; I wanted a beer."

"Oh," Jim said, disappointment clear in his voice. "I thought maybe you came here to talk about the picnic basket you dropped off earlier."

"Picnic basket? I didn't bring you any picnic basket, BooBoo. I really just wanted a beer...and maybe a little conversation." Jim inspected Jonathan's face and was convinced that his claim of innocence was genuine.

"Well, someone left a basket of nectarines on my back doorstep earlier. I just assumed it was you."

"But Yogi…maybe it was Ranger Smith," Jonathan said, then stopped what he was saying as if something had just sunk in and said, "Nectarines? I love nectarines…hate peaches though. Actually, I do like peaches; it's just that damn fuzz that bothers me…Ahhhhhhh!!"

"Yeah, I know exactly what you mean. There was a note in the basket too; it seemed like something you'd do."

"I'd never do anything so thoughtful without taking credit for it," he said with a sarcastic tone and slight chuckle. "Did you eat all of the nectarines or are there some left to share with a friend?" He thought for a second and asked, "What did the note say?"

Jim grabbed the card and handed it to him. Jonathan read it silently, thought for a moment and then said; "You found this on your doorstep?"

"Yeah."

"And you don't know who left it?"

"I found the note tucked in with the nectarines. Do you think there's anything meaningful here, or am I just trying to find a message in everything that happens now?"

"There *IS* a message in everything that happens, so what do *YOU* think it means?"

"I don't know...it could be so many different things. Is it a message from the *Powers* or something as simple as someone being thoughtful and leaving me a basket of fruit."

"Yes," Jonathan said confidently.

"Yes what?"

"All of the above. In a person's action of doing something thoughtful, a message is also sent from the *Powers*."

"I don't get it...the first part of the message makes sense. That's simple." Jim paused in thought and Jonathan waited for him to continue. "But the last part...why the last part? *Thoughts, Words, Actions = Experience.*"

"It amazes me how four little words in a note can send you into a dither, James. Don't always over think things. Complexity is an illusion, remember? Sometimes a rose is just a rose."

"Funny you should say that....because I found a blooming yellow rose bush outside my back door as well."

"A yellow rose?"

Jim left the table and disappeared into the living room. He reappeared with the basket of fruit, the flower and a brochure. "This yellow rose was growing alongside the house and there was a yellow rose on the letterhead of this letter. It's the only correlation I could make with the yellow rose," he said as he handed the brochure to Jonathan. "I found it in the stack of mail on my coffee table."

Jonathan looked at the note as he reached for a ripe nectarine.

"Jonathan, I never planted that rose bush...and, and besides, they don't bloom this time of year. What's going on?"

Jonathan slurped the juice as he bit into the fruit. He looked at Jim with an approving nod. "No, they usually don't, and this nectarine is fantastic! It's so sweet. You mind getting me a napkin?" Jonathan asked, temporarily changing the subject. He leaned against the back of his chair and wiped his hands on his pants and then let them fall in his lap. He smiled and looked directly into Jim's eyes and said, "I told you James, It's time once again. Your energies are so high that beautiful things are manifesting all around you."

"Damn it, Jonathan...quit talking in riddles and half-thoughts. Please give me some straight answers...time again for what?"

"Time again for so many things."

Jim shot Jonathan a piercing look.

Jonathan leaned forward and put his hands on his knees, "Maybe a story will help."

"Please, anything if it will help explain what you mean."

"There was a butterfly and a bunny rabbit."

"Jonathan!" Jim protested.

Jonathan raised his hand to stop Jim's protest. "Hear me out. As I was saying, there was a butterfly and a bunny rabbit. They were both foraging for food in the same area of the meadowland. The butterfly was flitting from one fragrant flower to another while the bunny sat on its haunches merrily munching blades of grass. The bunny politely asked the butterfly if she would kindly watch the winds and report any change in speed or direction. Having such delicate wings, bunny was sure that butterfly could detect a shift in wind direction before anyone else. The butterfly replied she would be glad to do so, but asked why the bunny needed this information. Bunny said he was expecting a storm. A shift in wind meant a storm was approaching and he would need to find shelter. So butterfly stayed alert as she moved amongst the flowers while bunny continued to munch away on the tender grass. After a while, butterfly's sensitive wings detected the wind change. She called out to the bunny, "Mister Bunny, the wind has changed direction just this moment." bunny said, "Thank you for your report Madame Butterfly. I must leave you and warn the others to find shelter as well. You too should seek shelter for yourself. You have such delicately structured wings and would not survive out here in the onset of the coming storm." Bunny speedily hopped around the meadow calling out to all other animals and insects, warning them of the approaching storm. All found safety before the storm clouds rolled in and showered the fields with much needed rain. Bunny contently tucked himself away in his own hole, knowing the happiness there was in this day, for his and butterfly's simple task brought all of meadowland creatures the peace and comfort that he knew. The End."

Jonathan," Jim said in a discouraged voice. "That's a very cute little story and all, it really is, but it doesn't explain what it has to do with me and this...*time once again* stuff."

"I thought it did a marvelous job of explaining."

Jim shot Jonathan a perplexed look as he raised his shoulders and showed his empty up-turned palms in front of him, as a gesture of complete confusion.

"Well, it may be only one facet of the many things, but you my good man, are the bunny," Jonathan smiled.

"I'm a bunny?"

"Well, actually, you could be either the bunny or the butterfly. Which would you prefer? They are interchangeable for the point I'm trying to take here. You are a messenger. Over the millennium, the Powers have entrusted some to express important insights to the world. There are a couple of names you may have heard of...Buddha, Jesus and his Merry Men. They were all given insights to share with the world. Unfortunately their words have been misinterpreted over time to suit the intentions of the few. Take Jesus' parables for instance. He used them as analogies to explain to people of his time, the powers that are available to all of us. But unfortunately, over time they have been misconstrued. Organized religions are notorious for having taken these insights and twisted them to fit their own needs and agendas. Don't get me wrong...sometimes it was done with the best of intentions, but unfortunately more often than not, those words were used to control."

"Jonathan, get to the point. Why am I a bunny?"

Jonathan continued as if Jim hadn't said a word. "We're all messengers for someone in this world and it's not limited to the spiritual side. Newton, DaVinci, Galileo and Einstein all enlightened the world of science and other disciplines with the insights they brought forward. Some people simply carry a message to touch a single person while others have a message for the world."

"Jonathan?!" Jim said, in an attempt to have Jonathan get to the point.

Jonathan finally acknowledged Jim by saying with a grin, "Give me a second; I'm almost there. Well, to make another long story just a little bit shorter...all the people I've mentioned were *bunnies* like you. They used their experiences to raise the consciousness of their fellow man and helped define and sharpen the view of the universe for others who couldn't yet see it. Most people can only see things that have been manifested into their reality. It takes the bunnies of the world to bring these things into awareness." Jonathan looked at Jim to see if what he was saying was making sense to him and then continued. "Newton, for example, didn't create gravity...it was already there. Rocks fell on peoples' feet long before Newton and Murphy came along. It's always worked that way...at least in this reality. But Newton was the first to recognize it as a force that could be calculated. And it took Murphy, a couple hundred years later, to postulate that the rock would most probably land on your foot. What Murphy didn't realize was it only landed there because he expected it to. I'm sure Newton wasn't the very first to study gravity, but he was the first to write a formula to explain his findings. And Darwin...he didn't create natural selection, he simply explained it!"

Jim interrupted, "So...back to what this all has to do with me. You keep talking about this, *Once again*... Please explain what you mean by, *Once again*?"

"It's time once again to try and explain how this all works. Jesus did it with parables while Confucius and others used different methods to get the message out. You've been asked to bring a message into the conscious mind of the people...once again."

"OK, say I buy into this whole, *messenger bunny – once again stuff*; what is it that I'm supposed to bring to the conscious mind of the people? Who am I to do this?"

"You bring forward what you know and have experienced. James; this life is only your latest."

120

"Clarke...What's his first name? The writer...you know; the guy who wrote *2001: A Space Odyssey*?"

"Arthur C. Clarke?"

"Yeah, him," Jonathan smiled. "Easy for you to remember."

"Where are you going with all this?"

"Clarke alluded to the phenomenon in his book."

"What phenomenon?"

"The huge black monolith that appears in the beginning of the book and telepathically teaches the apes self-awareness and how to make tools out of simple things."

"Yeah, but correct me if I'm wrong...don't those same apes also learn to use those same tools as weapons?"

"We are only to bring the lesson to the forefront. It is not our purpose to control people's karma."

"So you're trying to tell me that out of the billions of people who inhabit this world, I've been *chosen* by God or the *Powers-that-Be*, call it whatever you want, to be some kind of messenger with an insight that I don't understand or know anything about?" Jim asked.

"Yep...that pretty much says it. Except you do have the insight and you do understand. Besides, someone has to do it," he said with a disarming smile. "And don't get a big head about being the chosen one here...remember, we *all* carry a message for someone. And your words will find their target. You are to be a catalyst to others so they can build on your thoughts and experiences."

"I know my insight? I'm pretty sure I don't."

"It's the same message you need to deliver to yourself. Remember, you're searching for what you already know. Start by listening to your inner voice...it's a simple matter of tuning in on that level where all is known, where we are all one mind, one spirit."

"Josie told me I need to write...is this something that the two of you have concocted?"

"No, it's something the Powers, as you put it, have concocted. Besides, you've known all along you had to write or you wouldn't have been preparing for it by scribbling notes to yourself all these years."

"Does this all tie in with the note I received with the nectarines? *Thoughts, Words, Actions = Experience.*"

"When you turn your thoughts into words, your words cause you to act and your actions become your experience. Once again James, it's not rocket science." Jonathan thought for a moment and then said, "Follow me; maybe this will help…"

"Another visual," Jim noted as he followed Jonathan through the kitchen and out the backdoor. They walked out into the middle of Jim's backyard where Jonathan looked up at the black moonless sky. "Look up there, James," as he pointed up at the sky. "What do you see?"

"I see a lot of darkness - it's two o'clock in the morning for god's sake," Jim said with a chuckle, knowing there was a reason for Jonathan's question. "Oh, and a couple of clouds over there," he added. He then waited for Jonathan's response.

There was a long, almost uncomfortable pause as Jonathan said nothing at first and then admitted, "I guess you're allowed to tease me…I do tend to get tunnel vision when I'm trying to make a point, but remember, turnaround is fair play," he said devilishly and then continued. "There is so much more than darkness out there, James." Look closer…as Carl Sagan would have said, there are billions and billions of stars. There are also billions and billions of ideas and possibilities to see and explore."

"Oh, yeah, I see all the stars but I'm having trouble seeing those billions and billions of ideas. They must be hiding behind that cloud over there," Jim said with a grin. He was easily amused by his own humor at this time of the morning.

Jonathan raised his hand high in front of him and swept it from left to right as if he were opening an invisible curtain. As he did that, a whale appeared in the sky, moving with natural grace as if it was swimming through water. The whale was followed by a pod of dolphins doing what they do. Jim stared in awe.

"Too bad you don't see the possibilities," Jonathan said with a smile that radiated through the night.

Jim turned to respond to Jonathan's comment but found that they were now suspended in mid-air…Jim, some ten feet off the ground, and Jonathan four feet below him. Jim wondered if the air was swimming with marine life or if he was breathing in an invisible ocean. "Jonathan?" Jim asked in a hesitant, half questioning tone.

"Yes?" Jonathan answered.

"What's going on?" Jim asked in a contemplative tone.

Jonathan floated up next to Jim and asked, "Why do you ask?"

"Ah, well, maybe because we are hovering ten feet off of the ground!"

"It's just to show you what a different perspective can do for you. For instance, from here you can see that Frisbee you so masterfully placed on the roof of your house last summer," Jonathan said with a grin and then asked Jim, "Did you ever wonder why some things in your life just never seem to change?"

"I'm not sure exactly where you're going with this."

"Well, for instance, have you noticed that you usually achieve what you set out to do?"

"Yeah," Jim responded, knowing that Jonathan had a reason for the question.

"And did you ever notice that while your career goals are always met, your love life always seems to go in the dumper?"

"Yep, all the time. I just had this conversation with Josie. She says it's because I've picked the women I have to learn my lessons. I sure hope I've learned what I've needed to and can finally have a good relationship. It's time already."

"So what you are saying is, *It's time once again*," Jonathan said with a chuckle.

"I guess. But where are you going with all this?"

"Did you ever wonder why you keep making the same mistakes?"

"All the time. Josie figures it's because I haven't learned what it is I'm supposed to learn. Why do you ask?" Jim paused. "Jonathan, again; where are you going with this?"

"Why is it, do you think, you haven't learned your lesson?"

123

Jim just shrugged his shoulders.

Jonathan continued, not really expecting a response. "The reason those things don't change in your life is because you're afraid to change the way you think. Change the way you think and you change your world. "

"I'm not afraid of change," Jim said quickly, defending himself.

"Well, if it's not fear then it must be complacency. You've embraced the status quo. Congratulations; you are now thinking like an adult," he said sarcastically and then continued. "Children don't have that problem; they have a natural curiosity and they *expect* everything to always be new and changing. It's only when we start becoming grownups that we become creatures of habit and begin to struggle with change. We forget to continue to grow and learn. Change begins to scare the hell out of us because it takes thought and effort. Changing how we think takes us out of our comfort zone. But when we are willing to change our view of the universe...the universe itself changes."

"I always thought I was a real free thinker. When did I become a grownup?"

"Don't feel bad...becoming a grownup doesn't have to be terminal. You can regain your sense of adventure if you choose, but there will be a trade-off...there's always a trade-off."

"I knew there was a catch," Jim said as he wrinkled the corner of his mouth.

"There's that *creature-of-habit* thinking again," Jonathan said. "It is as you choose to see it." He paused and shook his head. "James, you can have anything you want in this world...but you do have to sacrifice something for it."

"Like I said, I knew there was a catch," Jim said as he now wrinkled his nose and shrugged his shoulders in defeat.

Jonathan continued, "You don't have to give up something you hold dear, but you do have to give up something. You give up poverty for wealth and ignorance for intelligence, but you give up something. You get what I'm saying?"

Jonathan's words grabbed Jim's complete attention. Jim said, "Interesting...go on."

"Remember when I said religions have gotten things screwed up along the way?"

"Yeah," Jim said, nodding.

"Well, this is one of those things. The universe works on a balance of attracting and repelling forces."

"Kinda like a magnet?"

"In the simplest terms, yes; but I prefer to see it as the balance of Yin and Yang. You truly can have anything that you want, but you do give up something in the process. For instance, you give up playing a round of golf to work some overtime. The trade off... you get cash in your bank account instead of getting sunburn on your bald head. You got that Corvette you wanted...and what was the trade off? That stack of cash you had in your bank account that you got from working instead of playing golf with your buddies. You ultimately give up something to get something else. It can be time or money or people in your life."

"Hmmm, that's an interesting concept."

"It's more than a concept. It's a universal truth. Here's an analogy you can maybe wrap your head around: You know that Corvette of yours has a transmission with a whole bunch of gears, right?"

"Yeah, it's got a six speed. Why?"

"Did you ever wonder why it has all those gears?"

"More gears give the car a better power/torque curve and better performance."

"Exactly! But what does first gear give you that sixth gear doesn't?"

"Well, it lets me get going quickly and easily."

"So what you're saying is that first gear gives you lots of power to the wheels, right?"

"Yeah."

"In exchange for what?"

"Oh, I get it...speed."

"And with the up-shifting of each gear you trade off some of that power for more speed. There's that Yin/Yang thing again. It's

125

the choice you make as you climb those gears. And you know what? You don't feel like you've given up anything because the raw power is no longer needed." Jonathan paused long enough to see Jim working it all through his thought processes and then he continued. "James, the same is true in all things of this world. With every choice you make, you gain something and you give up something. You give up living alone to have a family and share the company of others. You give up working a secure job you hate to pursue something that fulfills a part of your soul. You just have to decide what you are willing to give up in the process."

"How do you know this stuff?"

"We all know this stuff. You'd remember it too if you stopped being a goldfish!"

"Now I'm a goldfish? Where did that come from? A goldfish? You lost me again; you just got done telling me that I was a fuzzy little bunny, now you're telling me that I'm a goldfish! Which is it? You sure got a thing for animal analogies, don't you?"

Jonathan cocked his head as he raised his eyebrows and said, "You are still that bunny with a message, but you're being a goldfish because...well..." Jonathan stopped, searching for the right words. "You see, a goldfish has a very short memory. Each time it cruises around the fishbowl it thinks that it's all new territory even though it's been there many times before."

"So how am I a goldfish?"

Jonathan looked at Jim with a sad frustration in his eyes. "None of this is new to you. You've been through all this before...through many lifetimes, but you're not remembering the lessons that you've brought with you." He paused, not knowing if he should say what was on his mind. "James, we've shared many of those experiences together. It's time. "

A chill ran through Jim's body. He didn't know how, but he knew what Jonathan was saying was true.

"How is it that you can remember this stuff, but I can't?" Jim asked.

"It's not that you can't; it's that you've chosen not to for some reason. You've confined yourself to live this life in a reality with only three dimensions and chosen to not remember. I, on the other hand, well...I've learned not to put those limits on myself."

"That's *so* philosophical...but Jonathan, explain it to me in English, please!"

"God doesn't limit you, you do! You know what the truth is, but you continue to play out your little drama. You're the only one who puts those limits and restrictions on yourself. You can remember everything if you choose to."

"So why don't I choose to remember?"

"That's by your own design. There must still be something you feel you need to learn. You've made that decision based on what you were willing to give up."

"And that would be what?"

"That's something that only you have the answer to, but you're ready to change all that. It's time once again for that as well!" And then he added, "Or I wouldn't be here and we wouldn't be having this conversation."

"So you were sent to help me?"

"*Sent* isn't really the right word, but yes. I'm here to help you and in so doing, countless others as well."

"As long as you brought that up, you said everyone we meet is for a reason, right?" Jim asked.

Jonathan nodded.

"Well, I believe that to be true, but just who are you and why have you popped into my life now?"

"I'm here because you have chosen this and the rest doesn't matter. I am who you want, and need me to be."

"Come on, Jonathan! Give me a straight answer."

"I am giving you the straightest answer I can. I'm just a guy who knows what you need to remember. And if it weren't me *sent* to assist you, it would be someone else...there's always someone. But in this case," he said with a chuckle, "you would still be stuck with me."

"So you're not an angel or anything like that?" Jim asked; a little disappointed.

"You can call me anything you choose." He paused and with an emotional lump in his throat, he added, "Last time around you called me your best friend." Jonathan cleared his throat and continued, "Over time we've all been considered by someone to be a Guardian Angel or mentor. Some have even feared that I was the Angel of Death coming to get them."

"So I *am* dead and you've come to take me where I'm supposed to go? Is that it? But didn't you just say I'm supposed to tell the world my story? How can I do that if I'm dead? I'm not going...not yet."

Jonathan waited for Jim to finish and said, "Are you done? You have a habit of jumping to conclusions before a person can explain. It can get very annoying sometimes. It never ceases to amaze me that people insist on labeling everything, even if it's just someone who is willing to lend a hand. But to answer your question - no, you're not dead. How many times do I have to tell you that? "

"Ok, sorry. Would you please explain"?

"Gladly, if you promise to quit interrupting. First of all, you're not dead and I'm not here to take you anywhere. I've told you that before. I've been *summoned* here to help guide you."

"Summoned by who?"

"That's *'whom,'* and the short answer to your question is, you did!" He then added, "Well, the Powers that Be sent me, but only at your request."

"You keep saying the *Powers-that-Be;* are you referring to God?"

"God, Allah...the *Powers* has many names... all of them correct; all of them just labels."

"So why did you say you were the Angel of Death?"

"I said that I was mistaken for the Angel of Death. Besides, that's only a label, a gross misunderstanding really. You see, I help people accomplish what it is they've come here to do...we all do. The misunderstanding comes in when they choose to move on to another plane and I come off as the Grim Reaper when I guide them to that destination. I don't snatch them from this world," he said defensively. "It's always at their request. No tricks or anything like that."

"My question still stands. Are you real, or just a creation of my mind?"

"Define real."

"Excuse me? What do you mean...define real?"

"Is Africa real?" Jonathan asked rhetorically.

"Is Africa real? Where did that come from?"

"You've never been there, have you?" He took a long pause and then added, "Everything *is* as you choose to see it. You choose to either accept or reject a reality. So, you tell me...am I real?"

"So you're saying that nothing is real?" Jim questioned.

"It's real if you choose to manifest it to be. You know that. Did you ever have a bad dream that seemed to be real but at some point you knew that it was a dream?" Jonathan asked.

"Yeah..." Jim answered, knowing that there was going to be another part to the question.

"And...what did you do?" Jonathan asked.

"I forced myself to wake up."

"Why?" Jonathan inquired.

"I guess, to prove to myself it was just a bad dream and it wasn't really happening."

"Why didn't you just change the outcome?"

"Where are you going with all this?" Jim asked.

"If you knew it was a dream and you could change the outcome...why didn't you just change it?"

"I never thought about it, but that would be cool."

"Okay...if you could change the outcome of an event in your awake time, would you?"

"Just like that? I just change the outcome?" Jim said sharply.

"I just asked *if* you would change the outcome. The operative word there was '*if*'."

"Sure," Jim said without hesitation.

"Be careful of your answer. You better think this through before you answer."

"What is there to think through? If I could do away with some of the heartbreaks I've experienced in my life...why wouldn't I?"

"Because you wouldn't be who you are today."

"I'd be better, wouldn't I? I mean...look...if I didn't have those heart-wrenching experiences, I wouldn't be so cynical about things, especially about the women in my life."

Jonathan sat quietly for a moment, forcing Jim to think of what he had said. He then looked at Jim and asked, "And the tradeoff would be?"

"The tradeoff would be that I would be much happier and content."

"Would you really?"

"Yes!" Jim said emphatically.

"James, you're not getting it. If you hadn't experienced the heartaches in this life, you wouldn't have empathy for those who are lost or hurting." He continued, "You can't possibly understand what a person is feeling if you haven't experienced something similar."

"I thought you said a while back that no one can experience the world as I see it. So how do you expect me to know what other people are experiencing?"

"I didn't say that you could know exactly what they are experiencing. I said you could have empathy for them because you have experienced *something similar*."

"So back to my original question; where are you going with all this?" Jim asked again.

"Let's say for the moment you knew that you could change anything in your life; past, present, future...and you've already said you would change some of the more hurtful things...then why haven't you?"

Jim went to speak, but didn't have an immediate answer. He finally said, "I guess I didn't know I really could."

"That's bullshit," Jonathan said calmly. "You created them and haven't changed anything because you know that you need to experience these things just the way that they have happened."

"So then why have I been hurt so much?"

"Because you've chosen to," he said bluntly. "When one door closes another opens...we are always given an alternative. There is always that tradeoff."

"Jonathan..." Jim said, almost as a question.

"Yeah?"

Jim stared, frozen in awe, barely able to speak. "Damn it Jonathan, you make my head hurt," he said when he finally got the words out of his mouth.

Jonathan smiled, saying, "Good." He waited for a few moments and then said, "James, I'm just telling you what you already know. We've talked about all of this before, even in the last few months."

"I know. It's one thing to believe what you're saying is true in theory, but it's a whole 'nother thing to accept it as reality."

"Well, it's time you start accepting."

"Now can you set me back down on the ground? Why are we up here anyway?"

"Perspective, my dear friend, perspective! If you were only standing down there...well, it just wouldn't be nearly as much fun, now would it? I have a sneaking feeling the Powers aren't done with you yet tonight."

Chapter 10
The Wave

Jim and Jonathan remained suspended in the same location above Jim's back yard. Jim looked around, anticipating to be gently lowered to the ground at any moment. When that didn't happen he asked, "Ah... Jonathan, why are we still up here?"

"It looks as if you're being kept after school," Jonathan said whimsically.

"Why, have I done something bad?" Jim asked with chuckle.

"Quite the opposite, my boy. I think you are being given an extra credit project. Obviously the Powers have decided to extend your lesson plan tonight. Follow me." Jonathan began walking up an invisible set of steps and disappeared from sight before Jim could follow.

"Where'd you go?" Jim asked to an empty night sky.

Jonathan's head popped back into view with the rest of his body still hidden behind an invisible curtain. He smiled at Jim. "That expression on your face is priceless, Jimmers. The confused, furled brow look works for you, but you better stop it or your face will freeze like that," he said lightly and added, "Are you coming?"

"Where we goin'?"

"You'll see."

"How do I get up to where you are?"

"Magic," Jonathan replied. Then, using the same motion that a magician would use to levitate a beautiful assistant, Jonathan raised his opened hands, palms up, from his waist to mid-chest, raising Jim to his level. Although Jim's new perspective was only several feet higher than his previous location, it made him light headed and disoriented. He felt as if he had stood up too quickly and his brain was starved of blood.

He couldn't distinguish up from down, left from right, leaving him feeling nauseous. He closed his eyes hoping that it would provide a reprieve from the visual confusion.

Jim heard Jonathan say, "Are you okay, Jimmy boy?"

With his eyes still closed, Jim shook his head and said, "No, not really... When you raised me up, it made me dizzy."

"That feeling will past in a moment or two; or it should. I mean, it always has," Jonathan said halfheartedly, waiting for Jim to regain his equilibrium.

Jim opened his eyes, hoping to make some sense of his surroundings. He looked up at Jonathan and realized that Jonathan no longer had any physical form. Even though he was beyond physical being, Jim knew it was still Jonathan. It was like some dreams you have where you know who a person is without actually seeing their physical form. It was then Jim realized that he too had been separated from his body. "Jonathan?"Jim said in astonishment.

"Yes James, I'm here," Jonathan said reassuringly. Then he added, "You need to shift gears, Jimmy boy. Quit trying to make sense of it all with that damn left-brain logic of yours...give it a rest. Don't pay attention to what your eyes are telling you. Let your right brain take the lead on this one. "

"What's happening? I'm not liking this at all; I want to go back. Take me back, Jonathan."

"No way...not this time...I took you back to the drop zone you knew when we jumped through the doorway.... you're not going to back out this time. You're the one who keeps saying you want to learn, so get used to it. It's not like you haven't been here before," Jonathan said sternly and then softened saying, "James, there is nothing to fear. I'll be here for you, just like when we were together over France last time around."

"Oh sure, make a reference to something I don't remember... that's real comforting. Wasn't the end result of that experience me getting shot out of the sky and crashing?" Jim asked irritably.

"Okay, not the best example. Just calm down and shift gears, James. You'll be okay. Close your eyes; take a deep breath, clear your mind and slow things down. Use the lessons you've learned flying. Remember the first time Josie showed you how to make steep, evasive turns?"

"Sure. What about it?"

"Remember how disoriented you got when she pulled the plane into a steep bank turn?"

"Again, yeah... but what about it?"

"Remember how you felt when the horizon seemed to horseshoe across the windshield as you made those tight turns? Those were new sensations at the time and you needed time to process them. You had trouble disseminating all that input but you slowed things down in your mind and sorted through it and made sense of it all. It just took some time and some practice...right? The same thing is happening here."

"Sorry, but that's not helping me right now. You got any other bright ideas?"

"Actually, I do..." Jonathan quipped. "OK, try this... Sit back, relax and pretend you're watching a movie... Do you remember that classic scene in *2001: A Space Odyssey* when the director, what's his name again?" Jonathan asked, intentionally trying to change Jim's focus.

"Kubrick," Jim reminded him. "You sure do like that movie, don't you? But what's your point?"

"Remember the scene toward the end of the movie where all of those psychedelic patterns stream by on the screen with that eerie music playing?"

"Yeah, that was good. Impressive special effects, especially for 1968."

"Well, think of this as even cooler effects now," Jonathan said lightly and added, "Kubrick let you know that a transformation was happening even if you didn't understand exactly what it was. Now... let that same sensation wash over you; let it envelop you. Let everything you are seeing flow through your consciousness. Don't try to stop it, understand it or control it; just accept it as it is.

Don't try to '*see*' this place... Instead feel and become a part of it, like the aquamarine sphere we've previously met in."

Jim began to let what he was seeing stream by and as he did, he felt warmth permeate through him as he heard Jonathan once again say, "Something is changing, Jimmy boy. Can you feel it?"

"You are a master of understatement, Jonathan. It feels good, but I still can't make sense out of any of this."

"That's because you're still thinking about it. Think of this situation just like trying to understand a teenager...it's gonna take a while. Give it a minute or two and things will settle down for you."

Jim took in everything around him and found his surroundings in a constant state of flux. Colors swirled like curling smoke through rising currents of warm air. The smoke slowly settled into several horizontal bands. The top layer was a beautiful shade of blue while a band of a fluffy whitish color formed at the bottom. Separating the two stripes was a middle layer of aquamarine. These narrow bands gave Jim a false horizon and a chance to regain his orientation. He watched those lines define themselves, giving him an even better point of reference. The bands now ran somewhat parallel to one another. The middle layer began to widen and over a matter of minutes began to oscillate and took on a pronounced undulation. It shimmered and rolled as it continued to build, as if it were compressing itself into a monstrously huge ocean waves.

"James, you may want to get out of the way, or at least step back a bit," Jonathan warned.

It was only after Jonathan's comment that Jim realized it was indeed a gigantic wall of water. There wasn't time for him to move out of the way before the wave came crashing over the top of him. Jim was swallowed up by the wave as it tossed him head over heels in a deluge of saltwater. The wave subsided, going back where it came from, and Jim finally regained his footing. Coughing, he yelled out, "Jonathan...What the hell?"

Before Jonathan could respond, Jim asked "Now, what the hell was that?"

Jonathan laughed out loud. "I'm sorry, but I thought you'd realize what that was and would retreat to higher ground. You really didn't see that coming, did you?"

"How could I?"

"I guess you've got a point. I'm sorry, but it was still fun to watch."

"Yeah, I'm sure...at my expense!" Jim shot back. "Jonathan, what was the point of that?"

"Look around you."

"WHAT?"

"Look around you," Jonathan insisted. "That distraction was intended to change your focus."

"Well, it worked," Jim said with a chuckle, finally recognizing the humor in it. "But I still don't know where we are."

"We haven't moved. We're in the same place you were before, James, just in a different state."

"Well, it sure as hell isn't Kansas."

Jonathan chuckled again, "How do you know; have you ever been to Kansas?"

"No, but I'd put money on it that you won't find waves like that anywhere in Kansas."

Jonathan chuckled, "You'd win. And you are right, this isn't Kansas. You're in a state of what I like to call, *pure* form. Yeah, I know, I put a label on it but I had to explain it to you somehow."

"Pure form?" Jim questioned.

"You like to repeat people, don't you? You're a pappagallo," Jonathan said with a slight chuckle.

"Jonathan, please...."

"We are literally in the space between light."

"Excuse me?"

"Believe it or not, the light we see comes to us in packets call 'quantums'. It's a physics thing. It might even be a quantum physics thing. I'm not exactly sure but anyway, it's a thing that Einstein and his peers determined back in....in.....well, let's just say it was at some point before today. Again, it's physics at its finest. You can Google it if you don't want to believe me. Anyway, there is a space between these packets and that is where we are right now. I don't know how else to explain it. Within this space, we enter a level of consciousness where all is known. We're in the purest form that there is; well, as far as I'm aware of anyway."

"What do you mean, as far you're aware of?"

"If I knew all the answers I wouldn't be here talking to you, now, would I? The best I can do is pass on to you the pieces I bring to the party. And that is why we are all here. Most people don't realize THIS state of being exists. I'm positive; well I'm pretty sure…okay, I'm guessing that there are many more 'states' out there for us to find."

"Gotcha. So you're saying you are human?"

"Of course, but I don't limit myself to just being a homo sapien." Jonathan then changed the subject. "OK, back to the subject of *pure form*. Physics as we know it states that energy can never be destroyed. It can only change form and be converted or transformed in some way. There is always Yin/Yang going on."

Jonathan continued. "Let's go back to your car analogy. Step on the accelerator and a little gasoline is mixed with some air and injected into one of the engine's cylinders. Compress it and add a tiny spark to the mix at just the right time causes a violent explosion and the energy stored in the gasoline comes unglued and expands with great force. The gas has been transformed from a liquid to vapor, to a gas and the residual is heat. It's still energy, just transformed. In this state of being, we have been transformed into pure energy."

"But I don't feel any heat."

"Did you explode?" Jonathan asked, laughing. "Do lightening bugs explode every time they light up? James, you always want to over think things…just let it happen…enjoy the experience and see where it takes you. I think you'll enjoy trip."

"You sound pretty sure of yourself."

"Bank on it, Jimmers…bank on it."

"So what am I supposed to be experiencing here?"

"This!"

"This what?"

"Just THIS; clear your mind of everything else and just experience *being* for a change. You've been waiting for this opportunity since you came into this life and now that you're being offered that chance, you fight it and want to run back to what you know. Don't you dare run back to where you feel you are safe this time! Don't run back to your past existence without even exploring what else is available to you. Do you want to continue living your life wondering and searching in a drab three-dimensional world? Do you really want to continue living your life that way?" Jonathan didn't wait for a response. "James, empty the preconceived imprinted garbage in your mind. Don't try to make sense of this place the same way you're used to processing things in three puny dimensions." Jonathan paused and then asked Jim, "Have you ever done illicit drugs?"

"No..."

"That's a shame, but explains a lot. It's really too bad...you should have at least done some mushrooms..."

"Are you advocating drug use?"

"No, but it would have prepared you a little better for this experience. Again, don't over think any of this. Just let your true being tune into where it needs to be. Remember, you're not in a different place physically...you're just in a different place mentally, which is the only place that truly exists. Now open yourself up to what can be."

"But how? I don't understand any of this."

"For now, just clear your mind. As life's questions enter your thoughts, just let them go unanswered, without prejudice for now."

"That sounds good and all, but I have no idea what you mean by that."

"Okay...set yourself free from those questions tugging at your consciousness."

"But the answers to those questions are what I have been wanting most."

"Yes, but wanting is what keeps us from having it all."

"So I'm not supposed to want anything?"

"*Want* implies that we can't have it, whatever *it* is." Jonathan paused and cocked his head slightly as if someone was standing just behind him whispering in his ear and then continued, "Trust me again James; your questions will be answered for you in time, but for now open yourself up to what is here. Look around...see where you are and what you are being introduced to. It's time for the caterpillar to emerge from its cocoon and become the butterfly. It's time James; it's time."

Jim chuckled.

"What caught your funny bone now?' Jonathan asked.

"You just can't get away from those animal metaphors, can you? First I was a rabbit, then I was a goldfish and now I'm a caterpillar becoming a butterfly."

"And don't forget...pappagallo " Jonathan added. "I use what works. And you are all of them."

"I'll bite, what is a pappagallo, anyway?" Jim asked.

"It's the Italian word for parrot. They repeat everything you say. Don't let yourself be limited to your human form."

As the last of his words streamed out of Jonathan's mouth, the surroundings transformed itself back into a dark night sky. Jim looked around and realized that the stars had moved closer and immersed him in a *fluid* of glowing pods of bluish-green light. These where not so different from the aquamarine 'abyss' where he previously had met with Jonathan. The objects mingled gently, like the warmed wax of a lava lamp changing form as they brush against each other. They grew brighter as they encountered each other, pulsing brightly as they did so. There was a meditative hum that permeated through this new environment.

Jim sensed that these 'objects' were others in the same state of being that he now found himself. He was overcome with warmth, a satisfaction and completeness he had never experienced before. It was visceral. The experience washed over him, filling him with a sense of awareness that transcended time and space. He felt a sense of awe and a deep spirituality that couldn't be put it into words.

It was a sensation he somehow had known was possible and had searched for. It was the thing he had longed for his entire life and now it was right in front of him. With Jonathan's help, he had found it.

"Jonathan." Jim didn't actually speak his name, he merely thought it.

Jonathan responded in the same method with, "Yes, James. Isn't it a wonderful experience?"

"Are all of these...I don't know what to call them, these lights, people...like me?"

"Some of them, yes. The others are thoughts and ideas that have found their way here and are waiting to be transformed by someone's reality. They are also some of the guides you sense when you get that 'gut feeling' sensation before you do something....Angels, if you may." Jonathan added and then continued. "And every one of them is energy....pure energy. This is where it all gets connected."

"COOL!! It's so peaceful."

"That's because it's all positive energy," Jonathan added.

Jim looked down from where he was floating and saw his physical self standing in his back yard. It was as if he were having an out-of-body experience. A bright gold light trailed behind him, leading back into the house and exited the garage. It extending all the way down the driveway, diminishing to a dull glow as it trailed out of sight.

"Jonathan....what is that glowing, and where does it go?"

"The glow you're referring to is the energy trail left behind by the choices you've made so far," he said, as if Jim should have known. Then he added, "Tell *yourself* down there on the ground to take a step forward and see what happens."

Jim mentally told himself to step forward and the 'Jim' on the ground picked up his foot and began to move it forward and a circle about the length of a footstep lit up all around him. "Woo, what's happening now?" he asked, balancing on one foot with the other still in the air.

"What; the glow?" Jonathan said, playing dumb to what Jim was questioning.

"Ah, yeah...the glow," Jim shot back.

"That glow encompasses all of you possible choices; 360 degrees of choice. Finish that step and see what happens."

Jim went to step forward but quickly shifted his weight and hopped sideways in an attempt to trick the light. The light moved under his feet before they touched the ground. "Cool!" was all Jim

140

could say at first and then asked, "Jonathan, care to shed some light on this for me. No pun intended."

Jonathan gave Jim a crooked smile. "The pathway before you glows with a subtle golden light of possibility that's just waiting for our next step. The same choices may be offered again and again. It always requires a leap of faith but we choose when, or if, we are willing to take the path that is offered. We take with us the knowledge, experience and lessons learned from our past. If we are wise, we observe carefully and set out in faith, knowing that the Powers will support and guide our way."

Jim was still looking down on himself, half hearing what Jonathan was saying. He realized that he was 'connected' in both places. It was as if he were in both places at the same time. "Jonathan?"

"Yes, James," Jonathan replied with the tone of a parent whose child was asking too many questions.

"Jonathan, I'm up here and yet I feel as if I'm down on the ground as well. Which is it?"

"Yes," Jonathan answered and then expanded his answer, "You're both. Your physical body is down there but you are also in tune with your 'higher self,' which right now is here with me. I like to call it *being in the waves*'. Pretty cool, hey? With practice & experience we can tune into or jump from one frequency to another. We can even experience more than one at a time, which we are doing right now. That's how the prophets did it. How do you think Jesus could vanish and reappear the way he did? Know what the magician knows and it's no longer magic."

"Whatever it is, I'm lovin' it," Jim said, admiring the feeling that he was experiencing. "So Jonathan, tell me more about that trail of light behind me down there."

"If you were to follow that trail backward, it would lead you all the way back to your birth in this life. Think of it as picking up where your umbilical cord left off when it was cut and tied off so many years ago. If you follow it, you'll see all of the forks in the road that you've come to. And if that's not enough for you, it changes color along the way as well."

"Why does it do that?"

141

"It's an indicator of the type of energy you were experiencing at the time… like an aura trail," Jonathan said.

Jim chuckled.

"What do you find so funny with what I said this time?" Jonathan asked.

"I don't know…it just sounded funny to me. I got this mental image of the slime trail a slug leaves when it ventures across a sidewalk. I guess that's its aura trail. Care to tell me more about these aura trails?" Jim inquired.

Jim felt Jonathan make a mental gesture upward and they ascended even higher into the sky. From there Jim could see the trail much further.

"It's a time line of where you've been and how it's mingled with others' trails along the way. It's sometimes a bright vibrant color when we moved in a positive way, and a dim, dingy color when we've started down the wrong path. There are also times when we are tired and aren't ready to take another step for a while. It's what I call the mountain climber thing."

"What do you mean, 'mountain climber thing'?"

"When you start an assault on a mountain, or in your case, a new venture, you are energized and ready to take on the world. As you climb, that energy and enthusiasm wanes; you tire and find a place to rest.

"Wait - you used this same analogy before when you were talking about a person feeling the need to keep learning," Jim said.

"It may have the same starting point but it's about to veer off in a different direction. As I was about to say...from that high vantage point, you relax and view your world from a different perspective, one with a sense of satisfaction in your efforts thus far. But eventually you become restless, knowing that your original quest to scale the mountain and reach its summit hasn't yet been accomplished. That is when you begin to look over your shoulder at the next ascent."

"I hate to say it, but this is the exact same analogy."

Jonathan just shrugged his shoulders and said, "So what; it still works."

Jim nodded and in an attempt to make Jonathan feel better asked, "Is this why I'm always restless and never satisfied?"

"Those are questions only you can answer," Jonathan said but then added, "Albert Einstein wrote, *'There are two ways to live your life...One is as though nothing is a miracle; the other is as if everything is a miracle'*. As humans we choose to see everything as a miracle."

"Why is that?"

"Life would be pretty boring if we knew all the answers to all of the questions, now wouldn't it? That is why we are given curiosity. It keeps us interested in staying human," Jonathan responded.

"Now let me get back to answering your first question." Jonathan again stopped and grinned as he wrinkled his brow. "It seems strange that I'm the one trying to keep you on topic for a change."

"How does it feel?" Jim asked.

"Strange...in fact, very strange...down right, weird. Back to the original subject if I may. If, or when, you need that break, the glow dims and it goes dark and quiet. In the dark and quiet, we can listen to ourselves and think about who we are and where we want, or need, to go. When we move forward in the positive, the path before us brightens and each next step increases its light again to lead the way. It provides you with solid ground under your feet when you take that proverbial leap of faith."

"You mean to tell me it gives solidity to any direction that I may move?"

"Of course," Jonathan said. "As long as you are *in the waves* when you do so."

"Really?" Jim said, acknowledging what Jonathan had said more than questioning his comment. "But why doesn't it light the path ahead to guide me?"

"That my boy is called *free will*. The way I envision all of this, is we are offered only the next step when we are ready because our lessons can only come one piece at a time in this reality. Once again, I believe it's probably because the total picture would be overwhelming. It makes my point about trying to teach the second grader algebra before they've had a chance to learn simple math. Each lesson contains, as it must, the difficulties associated with each path we take. We have only this lifetime, as we know it, to learn the lessons....but maybe not... it may take several...who knows."

"Interesting," Jim said, soaking it all in.

"It's okay to dream James, as long as you build the proverbial foundation under them. You still have to put forth the energy and take the steps to make it all happen. Your little glowing path will always support you as long as you know *where* it is you're going; and *coming from* as well."

"What do you mean by that?"

"You have to know where you have come from to progress forward on a meaningful future. You don't wait until you are already in the middle of the jungle before you start cutting a path, now do you?"

From where they were perched, Jim could see his trail lead all the way to where Melody currently lived. He noticed that the golden light trailed off to a dark greenish-brown color. "What's with the ugly color surrounding Melody's place?" Jim asked Jonathan.

"Doesn't it speak for itself, Jimmy boy? What does it look like? It's an energy quagmire sucking the life out of everything around it. It was a good thing that you managed to escape from that mess before she swallowed you whole. She sucks the life out of anything that comes near her."

"You know, it's a lot easier to see the truth from this vantage point. Thank you."

"No need to thank me; you knew the truth all along. It's just made easier to understand when you can see things from a different perspective."

"Too bad though; she was wrapped in such an attractive outer skin. She could be so nice sometimes."

"Yeah, but even the outer shell she lives in is a facade. Trust me, she won't be able to keep her little charade going forever; her looks will fade soon. There's nothing real about that girl. She bleaches her hair blonde, wears padded bras and loads on the make-up, all in an attempt to cover up her inadequacies and low self-esteem. The poor girl doesn't have a clue as to who she really is, so she sucks the life out of everyone around her trying to feel better about herself."

"Well, she needs help," Jim said sympathetically.

"That doesn't mean you could save her. You can't save someone from themselves. It's their twisted path through this life. But I must say you did bring her into your life for some kind of lesson. Maybe it's to learn how to cut your losses and let go of a bad situation. That whole experience proves my point...be what you is, not what you is not."

"O-kay," Jim said slowly. "Where'd that come from, and would you like to expand on that a little for me?"

"It's a line from an old cartoon. It was about this little turtle named Tutor who always wanted to be something that he wasn't. And of course, there was a wizard who could facilitate the turtle's desire. Needless to say, each of Tutor's endeavors always ended in disaster. When that happened, Tutor would yell out, 'Help me Mr. Wizard' and Mr. Wizard would say 'tweasel-drysel-dreesel-drum, time for this one to come home' and he'd pluck poor Tutor from his current dilemma. The moral of the story every week was always the same: *'Be what you is, not what you is not. For those that is, is the happiest lot'*. It's a great lesson to learn at any age."

Jim smiled shaking his head, "You never cease to amaze me."

Jonathan shrugged his shoulders contently and continued, "Yeah, me too! But my point in all that is never back away from being who you truly are. Not believing in yourself is the worst sin...quite possibly the *only* sin. Don't allow those around you to form your thoughts and opinions. Believe that something *can't be* because those around you say so and it suddenly becomes impossible. Original thought is a rarity these days." Jonathan continued, "Contrary to what most people believe, inadequacy is not our deepest fear. Our deepest fear is actually that we are superior to those around us and that we possess unbelievable ability and knowledge. Our strengths scare us the most and we fear alienating our peers. We think there is something wrong with us if we are smarter or more talented than those around us. If you find that to be true, don't apologize for it...that doesn't help anyone. Do something about it. Go out and find those who can encourage and stimulate you to think even greater thoughts."

Jim suddenly found himself back in his physical body standing in his backyard with Jonathan beside him.

"Whoa, what just happened?" Jim asked.

"It looks like the Powers are confident you got the message, or they just had something else to do," Jonathan said.

Jim shook his head and smiled, saying, "You ain't right."

Jonathan just shrugged his shoulders and grinned.

"I was just getting used to being outside my body," Jim said.

"Don't worry, you'll have the opportunity to jump back and forth at will soon. But let me get back to the thought I was working on before we were so rudely put back in our physical bodies."

"Don't worry that those around you may feel insecure at first; instead encourage them to uncover their own truth as well. We are born with these gifts and it's not just in some of us, it's in all of us. As we bring forth the pieces and parts that we know, we inspire other people to do the same. As we move away from our fear, our actions liberate others to do the same. Don't try to take everyone you meet with you. That won't work, even if you'd like to."

"Why is that?" Jim asked.

"It's not your job. People must seek their own truth and we all learn our own lessons at our own pace. All you can do is offer them what you know. A baby naturally assumes the words you speak go with the object they think is interesting, not the object you show them. The same is true with people who are tuned into a different frequency."

Jim cocked his head.

Jonathan continued, "Did you ever notice some people can achieve anything that they attempt? They know that all they have to do is tune into the frequency that they need. It's like learning any new trade. The more you do it, the more comfortable you are doing it until it's no longer even a thought process."

Jonathan paused while looking at Jim. "I think that's enough for tonight; you look exhausted. You need a good night's rest and some down time to process all this material that's been thrown at you as of late. We'll talk again soon." And with that, Jonathan smiled and walked away, disappearing into the darkness. Jim went back into his house, locked the door, turned off the lights and made his way to the comfort of his bed once again.

Chapter 11
The Trip

Jim didn't know how long he had slept before the phone rang and woke him up, but it was already light out when he reached for the phone. He mumbled something that almost resembled a 'hello.'

It was Rabina, and she started by saying, "Boy you sound rough this morning. I'm sorry for calling so early and I wasn't sure if you'd be up yet but I just had to call. So much has happened since Saturday. I just had to call and tell you about it! I tell you, since you dropped me off at my apartment the other night it's been nonstop - people calling, and experiencing really, really strange coincidences. My good neighbor Chris heard about the accident at the drop zone and stopped by to find out what happened. He knew I did that kind of thing and figured I could fill him in with details. He was surprised to hear I was one of the people involved in the accident; he had no idea.

Anyway, we got to talkin' and he told me that he had been a paratrooper during World War II. He had been dropped into all kinds of unfriendly places across Europe... and get this; one time he was hidden from the Germans by some farmers who favored the allies; in FRANCE, no less...just like you!

Well, as we talked, we got thirsty and started drinking beer. And of course we started talkin' smart...anyway, we got into some really cool conversations about life and even possible past lives. I mean, come on, last week I couldn't fathom the thought of such a ridiculous thing as past lives and now I'm talking to my neighbor about that stuff as if it's common place!"

Rabina finally paused to take a breath. That was when Jim asked with a chuckle, "Who is this?"

"Are you serious? It's me, Rabina...you clown! It sounds like someone needs a huge cup of coffee."

"Hey Crash Buddy! It sounds like you've already had too much coffee. Glad to hear that your life has become, shall we say, interesting. I tried calling you yesterday but you didn't answer and then I got busy and kinda forgot to get back to you. It sounds like we need to get together and swap stories. A lot has happened to me too."

"That sounds good, but it will have to be today...in fact it will have to be this morning, 'cause I still have to pack. You see, I'm catching a red-eye flight to Paris later tonight."

Jim sat up in bed. "What? You're going where? Why?"

Rabina laughed. "Yup, I'll tell you all about it after, but right now I'll just say by chance I found a really cheap flight online. I think it's one of those deals where the airlines sell cheap seats at the last minute just to fill the plane. How soon could you meet me?"

"What time is it now?"

"It's almost twenty after seven on my clock, so it's actually about five after, 'cause I set my clocks ahead so I'm never late....well, not as often anyway."

"All I have to do is throw on a pair of jeans and a clean shirt and I'm good to go. Give me fifteen minutes, 'k? You want me to come over there?"

"No, I wanna grab a good cup of coffee. Would you mind meeting me at Java Joe's? I just can't make as good a cup of coffee as they do and besides, they have free refills!"

"As if you need more coffee," he said and then added, "Sure, that's fine. Meet you there."

"Ok, see you soon, bye," Rabina said as she hung up.

Jim got out of bed, put on the jeans that were on the floor and pulled a fresh t-shirt from his dresser drawer. He quickly brushed his teeth and was out the door in less than five minutes. It was about a ten minute ride to the coffee shop. Java Joe's was right around the corner from Rabina's apartment and by the time Jim walked in, she was already sipping her coffee from a bright yellow Grande-sized cup and had another steaming cup on the table waiting for him. Jim waved as he walked to the table, and Rabina stood as he approached. Her face was beaming as she wrapped her arms around him, giving him a big energetic hug. She was giddy with excitement.

"Thanks for grabbing me a cup of coffee," Jim said. "So, why are 'we' going to Paris?"

Rabina began to laugh. "I know it sounds strange and spur of the moment, but it just fell into place. I'm dragging Chris along with me."

"Neighbor Chris? Why?"

"We've always had a connection, even though he's a bit older. Not sure what it is, but it's been there from the very first time we met. He's always told me I reminded him of someone from his past and that if he were twenty years younger he'd make a play for me. You know, I think I could let him. He kinda gives me a warm fuzzy. I feel safe when I'm around him. Anyway, when we were talking, he mentioned he spent time in France during World War II and that he always wanted to go back and see where he had been - but this time without the worry of being in someone's gun sights. Anyway, we both decided on a whim that we should go. So, I found these cheap tickets online and booked them."

"Wow that was a quick decision."

"Well, yeah it was, but like Chris said, 'Life is too short to hesitate'."

"I can understand why he might want to go there and revisit, but why do you suddenly have an interest in the wine country of France?"

"After you told me about your dream with the guys in big black boots, I feel I'm connected to this whole thing somehow and just decided to let it take me where it will. Besides, it gets me out of town until things calm down a little bit around here. It'll be great; I won't have to try explaining anything to anyone...at least until I get back."

"Speaking of which, how long will you be gone?"

"We'll only be gone about a week. I'll let you know 'cause we may need a ride home from the airport; we'll see."

Rabina proceeded to tell Jim all about her conversations with Chris, and Jim filled her in on his visit to Josie's and what had happened with the nectarines and the whole backyard thing with Jonathan. The two shared details of their experiences as they kept refilling their cups with fresh coffee, even though neither really needed more caffeine. After they finished with their stories and answered each others' questions, it was time to go.

"Have fun and be safe. I didn't think to ask; do you need a ride to the airport?" Jim asked.

"I'm in good hands and thanks for the offer, but Chris' sister is going to drop us off."

They stood and hugged again. Looking into Rabin's eyes, Jim said, "I hope you find what you're going there for."

"I have a strong feeling I will…I wouldn't be going if I didn't think so. I have a sneaking suspicion it's going to shed new light on your dream too," Rabina said.

"What makes you say that?

"I'm not sure; just a feeling I've got again," Rabina replied

"Well, good luck, babe!"

They left the coffee shop together and headed out into the late-morning sunshine.

Chapter 12
The Connection

Jim drove home from the coffee shop thinking about Rabina's impromptu trip to France. It wasn't even noon and he was wondering what he was going to do with the rest of the day, since he had no real plans. He thought maybe he should jot down some notes while they were still fresh in his mind and then maybe grab a couple of beers at the local pub where no one knew about his little episode at the drop zone. He was going to keep his distance from the drop zone until he had time to think it all through and had some answers for the people who were there. He was glad no one had paid him a visit yet, because he wouldn't have known what to tell them. He wouldn't dare tell them the truth because they would think he had suffered some serious head trauma.

When he drove up his driveway he realized there was no need to make any plans. Jonathan's rusted pickup truck was sitting in the driveway next to the garage.

Jim pulled up, got out of his car and walked around to the back of his house. There he found Jonathan sitting comfortably with his legs crossed in a lotus position on the ground, rather than in one of the available cushioned chairs.

"Hey, what brings you back?" Jim asked.

"My pickup truck. I thought you would have seen it in your driveway. You didn't expect me to just appear here, did you?" he said with a jovial tone.

Jim just grinned, shaking his head. "What's wrong, my chairs are too comfortable for you?"

"I just needed to meditate a bit and I thought being on the ground would...well, ground me. Look over there, I brought you a little gift," Jonathan said as he pointed to a medium sized cooler near the patio table.

Jim removed the cover and found many bottles of beer packed neatly in ice. At a glance Jim saw an assortment of beers from Leinenkugel, a Wisconsin brewer. The remaining bottles were a selection of Samuel Adams, including several of their hard to find Double Bock, a very good and very strong dark beer Jim truly enjoyed, but normally only when he traveled because he couldn't find it locally.

"Good choices. Wow, Where'd you find the Double Bock? And what's the occasion?"

"You were kind enough to share your tequila with me at the drop zone and your Saint Pauli Girl last night, I thought the least I could do was return the favor. You could say I'm paying you *Bock*!!"

"Oh, that's a really bad pun," Jim groaned. "But thanks. There's a lot of beer here; and let me guess... you wanna help me drink it too."

"That's a fantastic idea; glad you thought of it," Jonathan said, grinning ear to ear.

"Well, as Jimmy Buffet would say...it's five o'clock somewhere."

"I'd be willing to put money on it," Jonathan quipped.

Jim started toward the patio door leading to his kitchen when Jonathan stopped him, asking, "Where do you think you're going?"

"I'm getting a bottle opener. Remember, these better beers aren't twist-offs."

"I came prepared. There's a church key in the cooler," he said with a knowing wink.

"Great, it saves me a trip. Now I won't have a reason to exert myself until I need to pee."

"I thought that was what those trees over there were for," Jonathan said, pointing to the surrounding woods. It worked for me when I got here," he said with a grin.

"They do work well for that, don't they? I always said that I wanted a place with enough property where I could piss out my front door. But I had to amend that statement and add... and not get arrested," Jim said with a chuckle.

"Well, you definitely have that here. What you got, twenty or thirty acres?"

"Fifteen."

"Sweet," Jonathan said, nodding his approval.

"What made you decide to pay me a visit on this fine day?"

"I had nothin' going on and thought it'd be a good day to sit on your patio, drink beer and talk smart."

"Excellent idea," Jim said, grabbing a beer for himself from the cooler and one for Jonathan, who was still sitting on the ground in the lotus position. Jim continued, "I just had coffee with my friend Rabina. She was the other person who 'bounced' with me. She said some weird things have been happening to her since then."

"Not surprising," Jonathan responded.

"She said there have been a bunch of coincidences happening to her lately and she thinks she's going to find some answers by flying off to France with a friend."

"Is she taking Chris with her?" Jonathan asked nonchalantly.

Jim's head snapped toward Jonathan. "I shouldn't be surprised, but how did you know that?"

"Lucky guess," Jonathan returned, with a grin.

"No, no, no, you don't do lucky guesses."

"James my boy, nothing is by chance and everything is connected. You are so close to remembering that fact."

"You are really something. You never cease to amaze me."

"Would you like me to stand and take a bow?"

"If you wish, but you probably can't straighten up after being in that goofy position as long as you have. You look like an over-sized pretzel."

"You underestimate me, young man, you underestimate me. Ah, wait; maybe I do need a little help," Jonathan said with a laugh.

As Jim began to get out of his chair to help Jonathan up from his position in the grass, Jonathan levitated off the ground about two feet, still in the lotus position. Effortlessly he unfolded his legs and stood on his own.

"Now, why doesn't this surprise me?" Jim said, shaking his head. "You just love showing off, don't you?"

"I just like reminding you that everything is possible."

"You know, I get it on a gut level…I really do. But it's hard to bring into my day to day life. It's like the first time I went to Venice and Pompeii in Italy. It just seems too surreal to believe I was actually there. I read about these places in books, complete with pictures, but to actually be there didn't seem real. It took a second visit to bring it into my consciousness and to know I had actually been there."

"You need to practice it more often. That is exactly why these events keep reoccurring. It's all meant to reinforce this IS real to you. Each time you experience something, it's easier to see more detail in what it is you're doing," Jonathan emphasized.

Jim nodded.

Jonathan continued, "It's always easier to accomplish something when you know what you are doing. It's all connected."

"By connected, are you saying confidence and accomplishing a goal?"

"That too, but I'm saying everything is connected. Everything you do is connected in some way to those around you. That is why you should always do the right thing. That is why those Ten Commandments were chiseled in stone a couple thousand years ago."

"Keep going; I'm listening."

"There has to be a balance, or things start to go terribly wrong. The Earth and the other planets in the Milky Way rotate around the sun and the Milky Way spins around a huge black hole; and all of it spins around who knows what. All the stars and all the other planets rotate around each other in just the right orbit to sustain their existence. There is a balance between gravity trying to draw them in, and repulsion to keep them in a measurable orbital cycle. Sometimes things do collide and for a while there is chaos, but in time a balance is struck once again. It's that Yin/Yang thing all over again. Tides rise and fall, the sun rises and sets like clockwork. Seasons are a rebirth and cleansing. A balance needs to be struck in everything you do to raise to the next level of consciousness."

"I'm amazed. I'm only on my first beer, but I'm still understanding what you are proposing here," Jim said chuckling.

"Atoms spin around other atoms, proteins cling together to make DNA; DNA bunches together to make organisms. There is an equilibrium and balance that is struck, with everything spinning and revolving around everything else."

"So, let me get this straight... You're telling me that for every good deed I do, I need to do something 'not nice'?"

"No, you should always operate your life from a position of using positive energy. Like any good super-power you should always use your power only for good," he said with a chuckle. "There is nothing positive about the negative. Don't get me wrong, you do have the freewill to run your life on negative energy if you wish but you will then live it like Melody and the many people like her. Believe me, it's not a happy existence."

"So for instance, you're saying that stealing is more detrimental to the person who is doing the stealing?"

"Of course…they are creating so much negative energy, how can it be anything but? Negative energy creates a vortex, a swirling caldron of negative karmic energy. It's not only one persons' loss. While it does violate the person being robbed, it also leaves an imprint with the person doing the stealing that re-enforces the idea that they aren't capable of earning a living in a productive way on their own. Stealing creates so much pure negative energy that the cycle not only continues, but escalates each time we do something we know is wrong.

The very *act* of stealing conveys to the person doing the stealing that they don't have the power to create the things they want...so they take it from someone else.

Stealing comes in many forms and isn't limited to physical objects. There are some like your old girlfriend who not only rob you of your money but also of your positive energy. They suck what they can from everyone around them because they don't believe that they can produce anything positive on their own."

"Wow, that's a great point," Jim noted.

"If you live your life in positive energy, you know that you can have anything that you want and in knowing that, why would we ever need to steal?"

"I never thought of it that way before."

"I know," Jonathan said with an exaggerated tone. "Buddhist monks believe 'wanting' is the only thing that keeps you from having everything."

"You're giving me a whole new perspective on the subject."

"It's like that with everything…cause and effect. Yin/Yang. That was the whole intent of the Commandments. Actually, there are 613 mentioned in the Bible. Each of them deals with energy flow and its repercussions if it is restricted. But the first ten are the major ones and got top billing by Moses," Jonathan said, adding a bit of humor.

"I thought the commandments were given to Moses by God as religious ideology or dogma."

"Throughout the Millennium, people have been lead to believe the Ten Commandments are a religious thing, but they didn't start out that way. Unfortunately it was the Catholic Church that probably first gave the commandments that connotation when they seized the opportunity to use it to their advantage. What better way to control the masses but to put the fear of God into them? The Church used the Commandments in such a way to keep everyone obedient or risk eternal condemnation in a fiery Hell." Jonathan paused as he contemplated a thought.

"I shouldn't be so hard on the Church," he continued, "They may have done it with the best of intentions; or maybe not. It may have just been how it was interpreted at the time. Whichever the case, they will have to deal with what they've wrought. Whatever the case, it's time once again to set the record straight.

The Ten Commandments were never intended as a punishment or to deprive people from enjoying life. They were brought down the mountain to help raise us up to a higher consciousness. By following those ten 'guidelines,' we are taught we can channel our energy in a more productive way and not waste it on negative things…like Melody."

Jim cocked his head.

Jonathan laughed, "I just had to throw that in there to see if you were still paying close attention. But it does make my point. That girl goes against most of the commandments and does nothing but suck energy from those around her and from the universe in general."

"So then, why does the universe keep her around?"

"Excellent question, and I'll address it in a minute, but I wanna finish the point I'm trying to make here first...okay?" Jim nodded and Jonathan continued on his original point.

"The first three Commandments deal with our personal energy and the last seven with interpersonal relationships."

"Wait a minute, I was raised Catholic and I distinctly remember being told by the nuns that the first three commandments pertain to showing reverence to God."

Jonathan let out a laugh of surprise. "That is exactly what the church wants you to believe. That is part of that 'twisting of the truth to fit your own agenda' we talked about the other night."

"Okay, so those commandments don't pertain to praising God then? Isn't it sacrilegious to even say that?" Jim asked.

"The Church actually has it half right, in a convoluted sort of way," Jonathan said. "Again, each of the first three commandments deals with our personal energy flow. They remind us to believe in ourselves and not give our power to someone or something else. They encourage us not to doubt our own abilities...not to doubt the God who is inside of all of us. You don't need a lucky rabbit's foot or your purple socks to get what you want; you just need to believe in yourself. "The Powers have put us in charge of ourselves and gave us the power of free will."

"As in, thou shall not put false gods before me?" Jim asked.

"Exactly! God is like a good parent; they give us the tools and support we need as we are growing up and then at some point send us out on our way. It encourages us to stand on our own two feet and take care of ourselves. We don't need to pray to false gods or idols to make those things happen. Self doubt not only is a waste of time, it robs us of positive energy and starts the cycle of more doubt and leads some to cling to false messiahs as they spiral downward."

Jim nodded.

Jonathan continued, "There are people who can't utter a full sentence without praising Jesus. That very action screams out the fact they have no faith in themselves even though that is exactly what God had intended for them. These Bible-thumping people act as if God will strike them down if they attempt to do anything for themselves. It's *so* not true, but of course, every last one of them will tell me that I'm '*channeling the Devil*' by saying that."

"Well...how do you know what they say isn't true?" Jim asked.

"What, channeling the Devil?" Jonathan snorted. "There is only a devil, or evil for that matter, if it is first in your heart. It's that monolith again...the information is all there in front of us; it's all in how you channel and use it." Jonathan paused as a smile came to his face and he added, "But if I am channeling the Devil, people still shouldn't get mad at me. After all, I'm not responsible for what I'm saying 'cause the devil made me say it!" With that, he laughed so hard it brought tears to his eyes.

"Like I just mentioned, I've been told I speak on the devil's behalf a few time in my life... Well okay, lots of times," Jonathan said laughing. "Anything that challenges their belief system must have spawned from the dark bowels of Hell."

"How do you know they haven't? How do you know that you are right and they are wrong?" Jim asked.

"They aren't necessarily wrong...these people are just operating on a lower frequency with a different perspective than ours and are too narrow minded to tune themselves to a higher one where they can accept something; *anything* new."

"You sound so sure of yourself. What if you are wrong? Aren't you afraid of the wrath of God for blasphemy if you don't have it right?"

Jonathan laughed, "The Zen belief is there is no right or wrong and that everything just 'IS'. Besides, I DO have it right! There are just some things you know are true." Jonathan chuckled and continued, "We are on a level where we can separate truth from superstition...at least more than our predecessors. We now know the earth isn't the center of our solar system. Galileo proved that and yet the Church wanted to light him up like a match for even suggesting such a blasphemous idea just a few hundred years ago. How dare he think that God would actually make something other than 'us' the center of His universe? What Galileo saw was not blasphemy. He dared to observe and conclude what the Church and others refused to believe even after being shown the facts. And there will be enlightened ones in the future to take us even further. Besides, if the Bible is correct, God is all-forgiving and won't strike me down with a lightning bolt if I'm wrong."

"I never thought of that. But you mentioned something about not needing to pray. Are you saying prayer is useless?" Jim asked.

"What I said was, you shouldn't pray to false gods," Jonathan retorted.

"I thought that prayer was prayer...what's the difference?"

"Praying to a false god is putting the power in the hands of someone else. True prayer taps into the higher being within ourselves... it's a personal thing. For some, prayer or meditation is essential. It's a positive action, so if you think it will help...it will! The very act of prayer, especially when done in a group can be very powerful, very positive...and positive energy is always a good thing.

Shamans gave little pouches filled with supposedly sacred stones and feathers to members of their tribe when they were seeking enlightenment. The 'seeker' was sometimes sent into the desert on 'vision quests' to bring forth the result they were hoping for. By doing this the Shaman invoked the seeker to put forth positive energy. Its intent was to give the tribe members the confidence in themselves to go out and find their truth."

"You sound irritated when you talk about the Church or these Bible-thumpers," Jim commented.

"Yup. Don't get me wrong... I know I shouldn't be too harsh on them, for *they know not*. I know they are here to learn their lessons as well, but anytime someone imposes their views on others or tries to sensor yours or bully you to abandon free thought, their thinking is flawed. This life needs to be lived with an open mind to new ideas. We'd still be running around in the jungles on all fours if evolution hadn't kept trying new ideas out on us."

"That explains why I was told by the Sister Superior that I was, and I quote: '*A sacrilegious pig and going to burn like a torch in hell.*' That goes way back to when I was in Catholic grade school."

"What could you have possibly said to earn that sort of tongue lashing?" Jonathan asked.

"Oh, she used that line on us any time we asked a question about religion she couldn't answer. Then when I was in eighth grade and knew the Bible just well enough, I asked her what gave her the right to condemn me to hell when only God had that power. She got so pissed off that she raised her arm to backhand me and realized that there were thirty-four other students watching," Jim replied.

"So, what happened?"

"I ended up having to copy a large number of passages from the good ol' Bible a bunch of times as a penance for my act of blasphemy."

"Do you remember what passages they were?"

"Are you kidding me? That was a long time ago and besides, I was twelve. I'm sure I just copied whatever it was she wanted without giving her the satisfaction of actually acknowledging what I wrote...*and,* I pretended I had fun doing it! I think that pissed her off too."

"Oh my, James...so much negative energy was flying."

"Well, she started it," Jim retorted.

"She may have. But do you think that Jesus had said to turn the other check just because he was a pacifist? Au contraire; he was conveying the thought that we shouldn't waste our energy on the negative. Don't worry about what has happened; stay on your course and go where you want to go. Don't bother with the people who are trying to hold you back. If you look at the bigger picture, you're the one who's put them all there in the first place...so move on young man, move on."

Jim pursed his lips together and nodded.

Jonathan grinned slightly, knowing that Jim was understanding, and continued. "Probably the best known example in recent history of the power of pacifism was Gandhi. He not only was the ultimate pacifist of his time, he was also a great public relations guy as well. He set his goal of Civil Disobedience and

161

went about his life teaching those who would listen along the way. He never raised his hand in anger or violence...and look at what he accomplished!" Jonathan stopped talking long enough to take a long drink from his beer.

Jim sat quietly, processing everything he'd heard.

Jonathan continued, "Now, getting back to your question about why the universe keeps people like Melody around. The universe usually doesn't interfere with free will. We can do anything we choose, but in the end we all have to pay the consequences of our actions."

"But I thought you had said the universe has lessons it wants us to learn and if we don't get it, we have to repeat those lessons."

"It does, but they are all lessons we set for ourselves before we came into this existence. It's actually people like us who keep people like her around."

"And why would we do that?"

"For the same reason we watch soap operas and reality TV. We inherently know we need some form of conflict if we want to grow and flourish in this existence. Experience can be a brutal teacher, but if everything were easy, we wouldn't ever be challenged, so why bother changing anything?" Jonathan asked rhetorically then added, "When everything is going good for you, you usually don't try to improve the situation...you sit back and enjoy it, right?"

Jim gave a head nod to the side as if to say, 'Yeah, I get it.'

Jonathan continued, "Richard Bach said in one of his books, 'You are never given problems without a gift in their hands...we seek problems for their gifts'.

There are always going to be people like Melody who refuse to listen. Trust me, she is not a happy girl. Unfortunately she leaves a wake of personal destruction behind her. She will end up paying dearly for her trail of negative deeds. But in her defense, each of us has put people like her in our lives to help us learn our lessons. We put ourselves where we need to be when we need to be there. Sometimes it's not a pleasant situation and we wonder why these things are happening to us. It is because we have gotten off our personal path and need to be set straight."

Jonathan took another drink from his bottle and once again continued. "Remember my analogy about shifting gears...how you lose something every time you gain something?"

"Yeah, and that applies to her as well?" Jim questioned.

"Of course it does; it applies to her as well as everything else. And why is that?" Jonathan prompted Jim.

"Because everything is connected; yeah, I get it," Jim said.

"Everything *is* connected. This truth isn't always evident from our perspective but in the greatest scheme of things, believe it or not, it really is. There is no chaos. It not only takes a village...it takes a universe! As Shakespeare said, 'All the world is our stage'," Jonathan said.

"I understand the concept, but I'm still having trouble wrapping myself around that idea...I'm going to have to think on that one for a while," Jim said thoughtfully.

"Yeah, you do that," Jonathan replied.

"Can we get back to something you said before...something about the old interpretation of the Commandments and it being another reason why it's time once again...to set the record straight. It seems you've inferred several times that I'm somehow the one who is supposed to deliver this message? You're joking, right?"

Jonathan didn't respond to Jim's question immediately, seemingly caught up in his own contemplative thoughts and not wanting to get side tracked at the moment. They sat at the table drinking their beers in a relaxed afternoon silence. Jonathan finished his beer and got up from his seat to retrieve another. He tipped the top of his empty bottle toward Jim's as if to say, 'Are you ready for another?' Jim looked at what was left in his bottle and nodded.

Jonathan dug two fresh beers from the cooler, opened them and returned to his seat.

Jonathan settled in again and finally said, "If it makes you feel any better or takes the pressure off your shoulders, you're only one of many, many messengers. Many have come before you, many are here and many are still to follow. You simply pass along what you've learned from your trials and tribulations. Write down what you already know; your thoughts and ideas, and put them 'out there'. Inspire people to think. Those who are supposed to get your message will; those who aren't, won't."

"Build it and they will come, right?" Jim said.

"Exactly. Those who are on a frequency close to yours will find it. Think of it as helping some of those standing in line in front of the movie theater to move up a few places, just as you've had help from others in the past help you get to where you are. Oh, and never forget there will be those who feel it's their duty to condemn you as well."

"Why is that?"

"Fear," Jonathan said bluntly. "They're the same type of people I mentioned before. Anytime someone comes along who threatens their belief system, no matter how flawed their belief system may be, scares the 'bejeeberz' out of them. They have spent years or even a lifetime developing something to hold on to and to make them feel safe and secure. They need some kind of handle to give them the illusion that they have control. They've created a neat little place where they fit in. They need to identify with a group. And without that…they have nothing."

"But they are being offered the truth."

"Didn't I just talk about Galileo?" Jonathan asked with a grin. "Silly boy, truth doesn't matter to these people…*security* is key. There are those who still want to believe the Earth is only six thousand years old and that it's the center of the universe. It gives them structure to their lives. They will believe what they want to believe long after being shown the truth. It also gives them '*an out*' when things don't go their way, you can't be held responsible… after all, it's 'God's will'.

We've all done it. We've all hung on to a belief we came to know wasn't true, but we still wanted to hang on to what was familiar to us. That's where kids have such an advantage. They are willing to change their minds at the drop of the hat when they are given new information. We should all be more childlike."

"Would you like me to throw a tantrum?" Jim asked, smiling.

"Very funny, although you came pretty close last night in your backyard. You were just as resistant to change, so don't play like you're wide open to change either, my young man."

164

"That was different," Jim shot back.

"How so?"

"You were showing me a whole new reality."

"And that is different from these other peoples' reality...how?"

Jim went to speak and realized the point Jonathan was trying to make. Jim nodded his head and said, "Point taken. I hate when you are right."

"No, you hate when you are wrong," Jonathan amusingly shot back.

"Just drink your beer and give me a chance to let this all soak in...'k?" Jim replied.

Jonathan raised his beer in to the air in a toasting gesture to Jim and then took a long swig. "We can be like children again if we are willing to listen to that inner voice we choose to tune out, or at least turn down as we get older."

Jim raised his bottle to meet Jonathan's and said, "Here's to tuning in and turning up the volume."

Jonathan then asked, "Remember the other night when we were in your kitchen, we talked about how when you turn your thoughts into words, your words cause you to act and your actions become your experience?"

"Yeah, what about it?" Jim asked.

"Keep in mind your thoughts are directly affected by your emotions, so they also affect what you say. So be aware of how they influence what you say. That in turn affects your actions and interactions with others. Your thoughts become you in a form you can see. How you interact with others affects your future and your future affects your emotions." Jonathan paused and took another sip of his beer.

"So you're reemphasizing what was on the note card tucked in the basket with the nectarines," Jim stated.

"I'm just reiterating and clarifying what's already been said...that's all. I think you're finally getting it! It all comes back to the Yin/Yang of energy and how we tap into it. But again, those aren't the only things connected. In this time-space, everything is a result of the Big Bang. All of the matter, elements, gases, you name it in this universe as you know it, came from the same source...the same beginning. We are connected to everything...every last bit, every last sub-atomic particle. We can tap into that endless energy if we would only open ourselves up to it and resonate at the proper frequency. That is exactly how we do things when we are using positive energy." Jonathan took another drink from his beer. "Boy, all this talking is making me thirsty, and I've killed another bottle," he said with a laugh. "It's your turn to buy," as he slid the empty bottle across the table at Jim.

"Well, you've helped open my eyes to new possibilities; the least I can do is open a bottle of beer for you...not to mention that you bought the beer," Jim said. He grabbed Jonathan's empty bottle and retrieved two fresh beers from the cooler.

Jonathan looked hard at Jim without saying a word. Jim responded with, "What?"

"I know a lot has been thrown at you in a very short time...but after all, you've chosen to make it all happen this way, now didn't you?"

"I tell you, there are times when I'm scared and question my sanity, not to mention I think my head is going to explode," Jim said.

"Think of your recent transition as the proverbial caterpillar/butterfly scenario...it helps," Jonathan said, amused with himself.

Again they sat in silence for a time, sorting out their thoughts and drinking their beer.

"You mentioned you were having trouble wrapping yourself around my explanation of how everything is connected."

"Oh no... It sounds like you're going to present me with another 'visual,' aren't you?" Jim said, laughing.

"No, no...but with your permission, I was thinkin' of maybe making an analogy to hopefully give you a better picture."

"Yeah, that'll work. As long as you don't make me into another animal again."

"I can't promise that, but I'll try not to...okay?"

Jim nodded.

166

Jonathan started, "Think of all this as a highway system. You have your busy Interstate highways and state highways; then you have municipal roads, rural county roads, side streets, private roads and finally your driveways. Besides all that, there are train tracks and boat canals intersecting all of the above. The main roads will take you in the general direction of your destination, but then you need to take secondary, less traveled roads to get you where you ultimately want to go. Not so different than life, huh?"

Jim made an expression as if to say, 'Sure.'

"All these roads are connected...you just have to choose which roads to take and when you want to start. Each decision affects your commute in its own way." Jonathan continued again.

"Now add in all those other drivers out there on their quest to get to their own destinations using the same road system as you. They may not be going to the same place you are but they are using the some of the same roads. You are all connected by way of the road you are sharing. You must all follow the rules of the road and trust in each others driving skills. You have faith that everyone will merge and mesh into the roadway properly to keep the system flowing smoothly and get you to your destination. All it takes is someone to make an impaired judgment call or a full-fledged 'bonehead' move and everything slows to a crawl or complete stop.

When you are driving you don't think of it in those terms, do you? You're just focused on your intended destination and not getting in an accident."

Jim nodded but said nothing, knowing that Jonathan was not done yet.

Jonathan continued, "The highway system works the same way as your life....everything runs smoothly until someone interjects some negative energy, hence an accident.

Once the accident occurs it takes time to untangle the mess, get the traffic cleared and a positive flow going again. It causes delays, stress, damage to cars, not to mention egos...the list goes on and on. It affects everyone who is on the road and even affects people waiting at home for their loved ones to arrive or business meetings that may not take place. It's also the first responders who are called out to the accident. If there is an accident...lend aid; it's good karma. Even in the midst of mayhem, chaos, disorder, pandemonium, and bedlam; positive energy abounds with victims helping victims.

Do you see how everything is affected? Oh, and to continue the scenario; add in the unexpected trains having to cross these roads at some point during the day or drawbridges going up to allow a tall ship to pass. It all adds to the overall design of the system. At first glance, it doesn't seem like all the drivers are connected, but they are as well. If one causes an accident, it's a chain reaction. You can lose time, be injured, or possibly killed. If everyone behaves themselves long enough, you get to where you are going unscathed. But my point is, when you are out there on the road, you are part of the whole commuter thing just as you are part of the universe....part of the 'everything connected' thing."

"Once again, you've given me much to think about," Jim said, somewhat exhausted.

"It's time to do more than just think about it, James. It's time, once again, to put it 'out there' and let it take on a life of its own. It's bound to inspire future generations."

"But, like everything else, won't it get misinterpreted?" Jim asked, somewhat defeated.

"By some, of course. But that's not your job. Your job right now is to get it out to those who need to hear it."

Jim looked puzzled.

"When you give someone a gift, do you also give them a list of stipulations as to how or when it should be used?"

"Of course not," Jim replied.

"Your message is the same thing. It is a gift, and like any gift that is given, what is done with it is not up to you. How others deal with gifts we've given them is not our decision...it's theirs." Jonathan paused briefly, thinking of a way to further make his point.

"Ok, your message is like a bullet in a gun."

"I knew you were going to use another analogy...I knew it!" Jim muttered jokingly. "Is this the second or third one so far today? I knew it," he repeated.

"What can I say? They help get my point across, don't they? It could be worse...I could be starting with the gun," Jonathan said with a loud chuckle.

Jim nodded with raised eyebrows and added, "I figured I'd have to endure a couple of them when I saw your truck in the driveway. Why else would you have brought so much good beer along with you?" Jim smiled across the table at Jonathan.

"You've got that right, James. Remember, there is always a trade-off," Jonathan quipped. "As I was saying before I was so rudely interrupted, your message is like a bullet in a gun. It's harmless potential as it sits there in the chamber, but pull the trigger, in this case, your words being read by someone, and a flood of new ideas and experiences are introduced into the mind of the reader. It opens up a whole new set of possibilities to them. But like any bullet fired from a gun, it can also be used in a negative way. You are putting it out there in positive energy and as the gift giver, that's all you are responsible for. It is up to the individual as to how to use the information and how it fits in their life."

"Yeah, I get it. I've found that to be very true with some of the books I've read," Jim said. "But I have to interrupt you here for a minute, Jonathan. If we are going to sit here and continue to drink this fine beer, I'd better find us something to eat or we'll really be *talkin' smart*...as if we aren't already."

"Actually, I've said what needed to be said and I've got all of my '*talking smart*' done for the day. I've given you more than enough to think about for one afternoon. And as much as I'd love to stick around and eat your food and drink more of this fantastic beer with you; I must go."

"Where do you have to run off to so early in the afternoon?" Jim asked.

"To another plane, man...to another plane," Jonathan said.

Jim looked at him, puzzled, "What do you mean...you goin' flying?"

"Not that kind of plane, my boy, not that kind of plane. I've got some catching up to do of my own," Jonathan said with a wink. He gave Jim a pat on the shoulder as he walked behind Jim's chair. Jim started to get up and Jonathan said, "No need to get up...I know where my truck is parked."

Jim got up anyway saying, "I'll walk with you to the truck. I need to stretch my legs anyway."

"As you wish," Jonathan responded.

They walked in silence to Jonathan's pickup truck. Jonathan got in, shut the door and rolled down the window. He hung his elbow on the window sill, looked out at Jim and said, "I think you should sit back down at the table, bask in the sunshine, drink some more good beer and write yourself some notes."

Jim chuckled, "That's exactly what I had planned on doing...maybe even take a short snooze as well."

"Now you're talkin'. That's a great idea. Rest up; you're going to need as much energy as you can muster once Rabina gets back next week."

"Why? What do you know that I don't?" Jim asked with a raised eyebrow.

"Not a thing."

"Well, there must be something or you wouldn't have said that."

"My point is that if you 'tune in', you'd know exactly what I know....so there!" Jonathan said, and then he stuck his tongue out at Jim like a little child.

"You're definitely weird," Jim said as he shook his head.

"I know you are, but what am I?" Jonathan shot back playfully with a wink.

"You ain't right," Jim said, still shaking his head.

"Actually, I *am* right...but it's fun to act like a child sometimes. It annoys the hell out of people." With that said, Jonathan started the noisy truck, put it in gear and drove away.

Jim slowly strolled back in the direction of his seat on the deck with a contented grin on his face. En route to his lounge chair, he detoured slightly into the house and retrieved a notebook from the snack bar. He grabbed another Double Bock from the cooler and finally settled into his chair in a somewhat reclined position. He pulled his bare feet up near his butt, propped the notebook against his thigh, and began writing on the first blank page.

Chapter 13
The Past

It had been a long week for Jim as he waited anxiously for Rabina's return from France. Jonathan had hinted that things could get a little crazy for Jim when she got back. Jim couldn't figure out what possible news Rabina could bring back to cause any additional commotion in his life.

He hadn't heard a word from Jonathan since his little back deck visit on the weekend, so Jim couldn't try to get any more information from him. Jim had tried tuning himself into *"the waves"* as Jonathan had called it, but he just wasn't getting any answers.

Jim wondered where Rabina was and when he would hear from her. He hoped it would be soon. She had said she'd only be gone about a week and it had officially been a week...yesterday.

Jim lounged in his comfy deck chair in a somewhat contemplative mood. He wasn't in any hurry to go anywhere and yet there was an underlying anxiousness...as if he had a wrapped gift sitting in his lap that he was waiting to open. He knew he should have pressed Jonathan harder for information when he had the chance, but he also knew that it most likely would have been a futile attempt. He knew that Jonathan wanted him to start finding out these kinds of things on his own.

Still, Jim wished Jonathan would have given him a little bigger hint before he left in his truck that day. A mere comment about getting some rest before Rabina got back and something about 'tuning in' wasn't enough and kept Jim on pins and needles all week. Jim now wished Jonathan had said nothing at all.

Jim tried to curb his curiosity by thinking of something else. He decided to give this 'tuning-in' another shot. He took a couple of deep breaths and slowly felt his muscles begin to relax. His mind started to wander as his body melted into the chair and he felt the UV rays from the sun slowly irradiating his skin. He had a fleeting thought that he should have put on sunscreen before he came outside and then his mind turned to those spaces between quantums that he had experienced with Jonathan. Those ideas slid away.

He slowly stretched his arms out in front of him and then over his head, arching his body, stretching as if he were a cat. He then resumed his original semi-prone position. His mind drifted to a peaceful country setting, complete with a farm house and a slow moving brook. He was cognizant of the fact that this was the same place he had seen in his recurring dream, yet he was well aware that this time he was not asleep. This time he felt he was actually there. He could smell the essence of the farm. In the distance he saw several people working in the field. He counted three; one with long strawberry blonde hair pulled back in a ponytail, gleaming in the mid-day sun. He grinned, knowing that his dream girl was now permeating even his day dreams. If this was a self-directed dream, he was going to take advantage of the situation and go out there and finally meet this young lady.

He started walking in the direction of the field and as he reached the tall grass, he heard his phone ring and he was sucked back to his lounge chair on his back deck. "Damn it, this better be worth it," he thought.

He reached for the phone and looked at the Caller ID...it was Rabina! That made up for losing his chance to talk to the girl of his dreams, even if it was in his daydream. He probably would have choked again anyway. Jim pushed the 'talk' button and said, "It's about damn time you called me! What time did you get in? How was your trip?"

"We had a great time and I've got so much to tell you, but we're not home yet."

"Well, when are you going to get in?" Jim interrupted.

"Boy, you *are* anxious to see me aren't you?

"Yes, I am. It's been a while and Jonathan put a bug in my ear that you were going to make my life interesting when you got back. Is that true?"

"Like I said, I've got lots to share with you...but you gotta wait until I get home. My phone is beeping at me and telling me that I don't have much time to talk before my battery decides to die."

"So, where are you?" Jim asked again.

"I was about to say, we're in Chicago and will be boarding for our flight home in a little while. Would you mind picking us up at the airport?"

"What time is your flight coming in?"

"I don't know exactly. I just sent you a text with the flight info, so jump on your computer and check on your end, okay?"

"I'm on it," Jim said.

"Oh, I gotta go. My battery is..."

Jim logged onto the airport's website and entered the flight information Rabina had sent him into the appropriate spaces, then hit 'enter.' The arrival time appeared on his screen and he looked up at the clock. He laughed to himself. "Thanks for the heads up, Rabina! There's no way I can make it there in time to meet you at the gate. I would have had to leave at least five minutes ago to do that," he said out loud. He knew he couldn't get there in time to meet her as she got off the plane, but he knew he'd be there before Rabina and Chris needed him there. After all, they were going to have to retrieve their bags after they landed. Jim figured he'd catch up with them at the luggage carousel.

Jim grabbed his keys off of the table by the door leading to the garage, climbed in his car and was out of the driveway in a matter of minutes. It only took another couple of minutes before he was cruising down the highway to the airport. That was one of the things Jim liked about where he had built his house. He had the quiet and privacy of living in the country, but was only a few minutes from a highway and about twenty minutes from any part of several larger towns. He felt he had the best of both worlds.

The closer he got to the airport the more excited he was to see Rabina. It had only been eight days and they were only friends, but this time he had an ulterior motive for being anxious to see her...but he couldn't tell her that, now could he?

Jim took the exit to the airport and made it through three of the traffic signals before finally hitting a red light at the fourth and final light before the airport entrance. Not bad, he thought...one out of four. The light turned green and Jim accelerated through the intersection and turned left into the short term parking lot closest to the baggage claim area. This is where he figured would be his best chance of finding Rabina and Chris.

Jim jumped out of the car and walked with a noticeable spring in his step. He knew he'd better tone it down a notch or Rabina would know he was more anxious to hear about what information she had for him than he was to see her again.

He walked through the outer doors and scanned the people milling around; he slowed his pace almost to a crawl and began a concerted effort to find Rabina. Now he wished he would have asked her what she was wearing so he could pick her out from the crowd more easily. He scanned everyone at the carousel again, this time paying closer attention to each and every one of them. A voice from behind him said, "You're not going to find me over there." Jim's head spun around like Linda Blair's in the Exorcist movie, but without the weird voice and green vomit.

"There you are!" Jim said as he turned and stretched out his arms to greet Rabina. "How was your flight? I didn't think you'd have your bags yet," he said as he gave her a big hug.

"We don't," Rabina replied. "I saw you pull up outside so I thought I'd hide behind the door and surprise you when you came in. I knew you'd be looking straight ahead trying to find us."

"Where's Chris?" Jim asked.

"He's over by the carousel waiting for it to start spitting out luggage. As soon as that happens we can get our bags and get out of here. So much happened in such a short time! I tell you, this trip was awesome. There is *so* much I gotta tell you." Rabina bubbled with energy.

"I'm glad that you had a great trip. Did Chris have a good time too?"

"Oh, *did* he! You're not going to believe all the things we discovered."

"Jonathan told me I needed to save up all my energy for when you got home, but he wouldn't tell me why."

"That is so cool," Rabina answered. "How did he know that? He was so right...you're gonna love what I have to tell you!" She bounced up and down a couple of times, clapping her hands together near her chest.

Jim giggled and said, "You are absolutely giddy. What is it? What am I going to love?"

"I can't tell you - not yet anyway," she replied.

"What do you mean, you can't tell me? Why? What is it?"

"Oh, you're going to love it...just LOVE it."

"Well then, just tell me already."

"Can't...not here. I gotta tell you about the whole experience for it all to make sense to you."

"Yeah, ok, but you know I hate secrets."

"Oh, poor Jimmy. It's not a secret. I'm not doing this to bug you, although it is actually kinda fun. We need to really sit down and let it all unravel. Chris and I even have a past life connection. I always knew there was something about him," Rabina said with a tone in her voice that now seemed more contemplative.

Chris waved in their direction when the carousel started moving. Jim and Rabina strolled over to him, and Jim shook his hand.

"I hear you had a good trip. Was Rabina a handful?" Jim asked, chuckling.

"We had a fantastic time," Chris said as he looked at Rabina fondly.

"What is going on between you two?" Jim asked

"We'll tell you all about it later. Do you have beer at your place?" Rabina asked.

"Silly girl, I've always got beer at my place. We live in Wisconsin, don't we?" Jim answered.

"What I was thinkin' is that you could drop us off at our apartment building so we could freshen up a bit and then head over to your place. We can have a few beers and get caught up, unless you've got a better idea," Rabina said.

"That sounds like a plan. And it's sounding like it may be a long night," Jim said.

"Have I ever told you that you are a wise man, Jim?" Rabina asked.

"Only when I'm providing the beer," Jim said laughing.

Chris looked at Rabina and Jim, and with a waving motion of his index finger back and forth between them, said, "I don't want to be a party pooper, but why don't the two of you get together without me tonight. I'm exhausted and I just want to get home and sleep in my own bed. Are you okay with that? I don't need to be there for what you need to share with him, do I?"

"Whatever works for you. I'm not the one who's been traveling all day," Jim said.

"Rabina, is that okay with you too?" Chris asked.

"Yeah, sure...if you're tired, I understand. I forgot that you're an old man," she said with a wink. Chris gave her a knowing smile back. Her smile let Jim know that much had happened in their week away.

They found their bags on the carousel and the three carried and wheeled the luggage to Jim's car and loaded all of it in the trunk.

It was precisely fifteen minutes from the airport to the apartment complex where they both lived. Rabina filled the entire time rambling with general chit-chat about nothing in particular. She didn't even stop when Jim pulled up in front of their building. Chris glanced with a grin at Jim and said, "See what I've put up with for the last eight days?" Jim grinned back, knowing that Chris had loved every minute of Rabina's company.

Jim helped carry their bags to their apartments and then proceeded home to get a few things ready before Rabina showed up.

The first thing Jim did when he walked in the door of his house was grab the half empty box of wine Rabina had tapped just over a week ago and put it in the fridge to chill for a bit before she arrived. He opened the pantry and grabbed assorted bags of chips, pretzels and snack crackers from the shelf. He found some bowls and placed each unopened bag in a separate bowl and carried them into the living room. He placed them on the coffee table and said out loud to himself, "Boy, I hate all these preparation details." He chuckled slightly, amused with himself.

He anxiously paced through the house, not knowing what to do with himself until Rabina showed up. He absentmindedly opened the refrigerator several times, not really looking to get anything. The minutes dragged by until he finally heard Rabina pull up his driveway and park her car.

Jim met her at the door. "Where have you been, young lady?" he said, jokingly.

Rabina responded with, "France. It's nice to see you too!" She then made a funny face and stuck her tongue out at him.

"Come on in; what would you like to drink? I've got water, soda, beer and your favorite box wine chilling in the fridge."

"I got really spoiled with all the good wine they served me while I was in France. They managed to make me a wine snob in less than a week," she said laughing.

"So....what would you like to drink? And please don't make me repeat the list again. Come on girl, decide so we can park our butts on the couch and you can start telling me about your trip."

"Okay, okay, I'll start with a beer."

"Atta girl," Jim said. He reached in the crisper drawer of the fridge, retrieved a Bud Light, placed it in an insulated beer holder, and handed it to Rabina.

Rabina reached for it and said, "Je vous remercie! That means '*thank you*' in French."

"Oh god, am I going to have to listen to you spouting out French words all night long too?" Jim groaned.

"Probably," she answered.

Jim led her into the living room and they quickly made themselves comfortable on the couch.

Rabina looked at the individual bags of munchies in their separate bowls on the table. She smiled saying, "Boy, you went all out on the party favors, didn't you?"

Jim grinned. "Hey, nothing but the best for my good friend. I thought of also throwing confetti and a few streamers when you walked in the door, but thought it might be a bit much. I didn't want to go over do it; you were only gone a week."

"Thanks...I really do appreciate the effort, expense and forethought." She took a drink from her beer and then turned to Jim and said, "Okay, I'm ready to tell you about the whole trip. It seems as if it was a lot longer than just a week...it feels like a lifetime in some ways."

"It's obvious you had a good time while you were there, but did you find the answers you were hoping to find? And what's going on between you and Chris?"

"I sure did find some answers...and then some. Also, Chris and I found that we had a connection as well," Rabina replied with a sparkle in her eyes.

"Well, let's hear all about it then."

"After we landed in Paris and got unpacked, we grabbed a cab and did some of your typical sight-seeing. We cruised past the Eiffel Tower and Arch de Triumph. After lunch we decided to rest up for the next day so we called it a night. The next morning we grabbed a quick breakfast, jumped on a train and headed for Riems, a town about 80 miles east of Paris in the Champagne-Adenine region. That was where Chris had hid out in the farm house after he was separated from the rest of his paratrooper company.

He was so funny when we got off the train in Riems; he was like a little kid. He expected that it was going to look like it did when he was there in 1944. Boy, was he surprised!" Rabina said laughing and then added, "In his defense, he later said that he never stopped to think about how the area might have changed over time."

Jim just smiled, letting Rabina re-live the moment in her mind.

Rabina continued, "After her brief and private reminiscence, she resumed her travel recap. "Once Chris got over the initial shock of the changes and we got our bearings straight, we rented one of those cute little French mini cars – a Citroen C2, I think it was... and we headed in the general direction where Chris said he had stayed. We drove for a while and the further away from the city we got, the more I felt this strange familiarity with the landscape, as if I had been there before and vaguely knew where I was...and yet I didn't.

We drove most of the morning, but all of a sudden I pointed to the left, nearly poking Chris in the eye, and told him to turn down a road. When he asked why, I told him that for some reason I just knew we'd find the farm house nearby, in that direction.

We traveled the winding curves and rolling hills of that road for about mile or so...and as we came around a big sweeping left-hand curve and cleared a wooded area, there sat the vineyard in all its glory! Chris looked at me in amazement and asked how I knew. All I could tell him was that I *'just did'*. But what was freaky was I knew exactly what the house was going to look like too....even the inside!"

"How did you know?" Jim asked.

"Like I said, I just did. I'll get to that in just a little bit." Rabina paused and took a drink of her beer and then continued. "Chris said the place looked exactly as he remembered it."

"So then what did you do?" Jim asked.

"We drove down the long driveway to the quaint old, and I mean *old,* farm. There were several out-buildings and the well-kept house. Chris acted like a little kid at Christmas, as we walked up to the door and pulled a hemp rope connected to three separate bells. A middle-aged woman answered the door."

Jim interrupted, saying, "Oh, so she was your age."

"Jerk! You could have just let that slide, but no, you had to make that comment, didn't you?" she said, chuckling. "Let's say that she was *our* age!!" Rabina stuck her tongue out at Jim for the second time that evening. Jim smiled.

Rabina continued, "Chris tried to explained, in his very limited and rusty French, who he was and why we were there. Luckily, she spoke fluent English and invited us in and treated us instantly like we were family. Her name was Claire and she was proud of the fact the house, property and working vineyard had been in the family for over a hundred and twenty years.

She asked us to come and join her on what I would call the back patio. She excused herself for a moment and reappeared minutes later carrying not one, but *three* bottles of champagne. I mean, the real thing; they made it right there!!"

"I hear it's a little better than that stuff in the box. Don't forget, I've got it chilling in the fridge for that very moment when you decide you want it," Jim interjected.

"Very funny. Please keep in mind that when I drank that box stuff, we had just plummeted to our deaths and all the other good stuff that happened that day."

"Duly noted," Jim said, nodding his head.

"Claire shared with us stories about her grandparents that her mother had passed on to her. Stories about how they made it through the German occupation and their involvement as part of the French resistance. How they hid allied forces from the Germans and then helped the men get back over the border to the safety of England.

Anyway, Chris and I listened to her stories as we proceeded to get a little toasted on the champagne. I mean, we hadn't had anything to eat since breakfast, so the champagne was going straight to our heads. We looked at each other and knew that we were having a 'moment' and this was a great time. Everything seemed just right. And then to make a good time even better, Claire's housekeeper must have realized that we needed something in our stomachs and brought out a tray with fresh bread, cheese and grapes for us to munch on. They were marvelous, but I noticed Claire and the housekeeper kept looking at me very strangely."

Jim interrupted saying, "Now I'm going to interrupt and tell you to get to the good stuff already! It's not so easy when the shoe is on the other foot, is it?"

Rabina gave Jim a crooked smile and shrugged her shoulders. "I thought I was hitting all of the high points pretty well. It's not easy telling a story when someone is waiting to hear something in particular. Okay, here goes the Reader's Digest/Clifts Notes version...Claire is the granddaughter of the people who hid Chris...and *you*; back when you were a British fly-boy. It just so happened that while Chris was hiding out, he had a little 'fling' with one of their daughters. You may have slept with her too! That was Claire's free-spirited aunt Monique...who, it turns out, everyone thinks was me, last time around! So indirectly, you and I may have done the 'nasty' together... in our past life anyway. Weird, huh? I'll get back to all that in a moment.

But first I gotta tell you that it ends up that both of Claire's grandparents, her aunt Monique, along with another aunt and a certain British fly-boy, were shot and killed when the German Gestapo raided the vineyard. Claire's mom happened to be in town getting supplies when the Nazis showed up, so she was the only one in the family who survived.

It all happened just a few weeks after Chris had been there." Rabina paused and looked at a stunned and speechless Jim. Then she added with a grin, "Was that the 'good stuff' that you wanted to hear?"

Jim sat in silence for a brief moment and then asked with the slightest of smiles, "Do you really think we did the 'nasty'? I wonder if we were any good?"

Rabina rolled her eyes, smiling. "You men are all alike."

"Yeah, we are...and your point?" Jim said, pretending he didn't understand.

"Let me get back to the story. It's the part I think you are going to find most interesting. But first...I have to go to the bathroom."

"Hey," Jim said, "Making me wait is just plain old mean! That's it, no more beer for you until you finish your story."

"If you wouldn't have been such a 'guy,' I would have finished. ell, actually I still would have had to go to the bathroom. Be right back."

"Hurry!" Jim finally said after Rabina had already closed the main bath door.

While Rabina was gone, Jim had a flash. It was a glimpse of a vineyard scene, like the one he had had earlier in the day, just before Rabina called from Chicago. It was a clear picture of the life he had once known. In that scene was a house, the surrounding vineyard and his 'strawberry blonde' standing in a field filled with vines. That scene disappeared as he heard Rabina come back into the living room.

"Was that quick enough for you?" she asked.

"Yvonne."

"What?" Rabina asked, confused

"Her name was Yvonne," Jim said.

"Did I miss something while I was in the bathroom? Who's Yvonne?"

"Claire's other aunt, the one who was killed along with the rest of us."

"Oh yeah, *that* Yvonne. How do you know that?"

"While you were in the bathroom I had some sort of flashback. The house you were at, it was field stone with a red tile roof and matching shutters with two fireplace chimneys, both covered in ivy; one on each side of a huge half-round window on the back gable, wasn't it?"

"Yeah...exactly! How did you..." Rabina's voice trailed off as her eyes widened, "You remember being there, don't you? Of course you do, or you wouldn't have just described the house to a tee. What made you suddenly know?"

"I'm not sure. All of a sudden this perfect picture of the house and the surrounding vineyard just popped into my head, along with my strawberry blonde, and her name was Yvonne."

"That is so cool! Now I gotta finish telling you the rest of what happened that day. Claire decided we should sit out on the veranda on the west side of the house, overlooking the vineyard, to watch the sunset. As we walked through the house, I started telling Claire about the hidden room."

Jim interrupted, "Wait, you were telling Claire this stuff or was she was telling you?"

"I was telling her!"

"How did you know?"

"That's what I was getting at... I just somehow knew. I even showed Claire how to unlatch a hidden door where her grandparents hid guys like Chris and you. That was when Claire told me that from the instant she saw me get out of the car, she knew I had been her aunt Monique. Even the housekeeper recognized how much I looked like Monique that she had to do a double-take when she saw me. Remember I told you that she had given me a strange look when we met?"

"Yes, you did...just before I interrupted you," Jim said, grinning.

"Anyway, Claire brought us into the formal living room to show us a huge, almost mural-sized photo of Claire's mom, her aunt Yvonne, and aunt Monique; the family's three daughters. And I was shocked! I look so much like Monique! Claire and Chris said I even have the same mannerisms. Chris said there was something magical about her and he saw those same qualities in me the first time we met. He said he had actually thought of returning to France after the war to find and marry Monique. I think that's why he and I have such a connection, this time around."

There was finally a lull in the conversation and both Jim and Rabina sat quietly, each caught up in their own thoughts.

Rabina broke the silence saying, "I had planned on coming over tonight and partying it up a little bit, but I realize with the jet lag and all that, I'm really tired and need to sleep. Would you mind if we talk more about this another time, maybe tomorrow? I didn't realize how tired I was until now. I'm exhausted and just want to crawl in to my own comfy bed and crash for eight or ten hours...OK?"

"I'm sorry, I was so looking forward to what you had to tell me that I didn't even stop to think that you might be tired. I should have realized that with all the traveling and, like you said, jet lag that you'd be wanting to sleep."

They got up from the couch and made their way to the back door. As they walked through the kitchen, Jim opened the fridge door and pulled the box of wine from the top shelf and tried to tuck it under Rabina's arm.

"What are you doing?" Rabina asked.

"You might be thirsty when you wake up," Jim smiled.

"And you think that the first thing I'm going to want to drink is box wine?" Rabina asked, chuckling.

"Well, actually I figured you were too tired to give it much thought and I'd send you home with it before it sunk in."

"Nice try, cowboy! Why don't you keep it here for safe keeping, for the next time we have as much excitement as we did a couple weeks ago." Rabina paused with a strange introspective look on her face.

"What's wrong?" Jim asked.

"Two weeks. So much has happened in the last two weeks. It seems like a whole lifetime has been packed into ten or eleven days! And somehow it all seems normal. Think of it; in the last two weeks I went from watching re-runs on cable TV at night to falling to our death, flying off to France and finding out I was a somewhat morally loose French socialite who had an affair with my neighbor. If you would have tried to tell me that back a few weeks ago, I would have told you that you were nuts! Well, nuttier than you usually are."

"I know," was all Jim could think to say at the moment. He nodded his head then added, "But it beats watching re-runs, doesn't it?"

Rabina smiled and said, "Good night Gracie." She hugged Jim, placed the box of wine on the counter top and headed out the door with a wave and a smile.

Jim sat back in his favorite chair, letting his mind wander back to the house and fields of France. He vividly saw everything around him as if he were recalling a memory and not just imagining what it might have been like to be there. He saw his Yvonne, with her long flowing hair, walking to meet him at the field's edge.

Suddenly he found himself lying on a cot in a small room with tiny windows placed high on the wall, then hearing a commotion outside. The air filled with the sound of gun fire. Jim scrambled to his feet just as the door to his once hidden sanctuary was kicked open by angry black boots. Three men burst through the doorway. Instantly, everything slowed to super slow-motion as Jim became aware of even the tiniest detail. All three men wore the grayish wool uniforms of the Gestapo SS. Each held a machine gun and wore the distinctive German helmets which flared out at the bottom, red swastika armbands on their left sleeves and black boots with small horizontal chrome buckles on the side near the top.

Jim looked directly into the barrels of the guns and could smell the spent gun power from their use on what he had heard outside. The emotionless trio took another step in to the room and without any hesitation took aim and pulled the triggers, unleashing a spray of lead bullets in his direction. He noticed one soldier in particular, the one in the middle, and wondering if he was even old enough to have ever shaved. Jim tracked one bullet in particular as it exited the barrel of the young man's gun as it made its' way directly toward his head. He wanted it to be a just a very bad dream and wondered how much it was going to hurt when the bullet hit him...then everything went dark.

Jim was jerked awake in his chair, now soaked in his perspiration, by a voice calling out to him. It wasn't just a voice in his head. It was an actual voice that came from outside him and seemed to fill the room. He was well aware that he was now indeed very awake. He also knew he wasn't having a psychotic moment, as he had feared in the past. This was real. The voice was feminine and didn't actually call him by name, but she was asking him to visit Josie.

Jim at first passed it off as a residual effect from the bad dream he had just had, but the voice was familiar. It wasn't Josie's voice but he knew he had heard the voice somewhere.

He looked at the clock and saw it was already closing in on 11pm, too late to drive over and just 'drop in' on Josie, although she was a night owl and would probably still be up. He rationalized that if he got a good night's sleep and heard the voice again in the morning, he would follow the instructions and visit Josie.

He went to bed, tossing and turning for a long time before finally falling asleep. He didn't remember dreaming that night.

Chapter 14
The Future

Jim woke early and was still lazing in bed when he heard that familiar voice speak to him again. It wasn't a commanding voice, but sweet and soft. It was definitely feminine, and one he knew he'd heard somewhere before; he just couldn't place it yet. She again asked him to visit Josie.

So many bizarre things had happened to him over the course of the last few months that having a voice request he pay a friend a visit no longer seemed odd. He recalled Jonathan telling him everything he heard and experienced should be considered omens and a chance to change the path he was on in this world. Jim knew he should honor the request and visit Josie. He hadn't talked to her in over a week and if nothing else, he would catch her up on what Rabina had discovered on her recent trip to France.

He thought about calling ahead, but the voice said to visit. Jim knew too of Josie's dislike of phones and preferred to talk face to face.

He climbed out of bed, dressed quickly, poured himself a cup of day-old black coffee and popped it in the microwave for two minutes. He then poured the steaming hot java into a travel mug, grabbed the keys to his car and headed out in the direction of Josie's house.

Jim sipped his coffee as he drove in silence. He was looking forward to catching up with Josie. She always made him feel comfortable whenever he paid her a visit. He wondered why he didn't do it more often. His head was full of thoughts and ideas so it took him quite a while before he realized he hadn't even turned the radio; he obviously didn't need it today.

It took twenty minutes for Jim to reach Josie's driveway. He turned in and drove up as he always did but this time his eyes darted from one thing to another, looking for the reason the voice had told him to come.

A cold shiver ran briefly through his body with the thought of finding her dead on the floor. Was that why the voice was beckoning him to visit instead of simply calling? He was relieved when he saw Josie standing by the kitchen window over the sink. He realized he had stopped breathing when the thought of finding her dead had struck him. Now he could finally breathe again.

Josie gave Jim a curious look as he parked the car and walked toward the porch. Josie wiped her hands on her apron and opened the screen door. She had an expression on her face he had never seen before. "You know, I tend to see a person's present life and what brought them to this point. I even get flashes of their future, but I have to admit I really didn't see this one coming."

"You didn't see what coming? You look pale. Josie, are you okay?" Jim asked.

"Oh, I'm *better* than okay, much better. In fact I'm delighted!"

"By what?"

"My granddaughter Shelby and I spent a wonderful weekend together. We talked about things we'd never shared before. We hit on all kinds of subjects neither one of us had ever brought up in the past because we didn't think the other had any interest in them." Josie stopped talking and looked at Jim with a huge smile and a sparkle in her glossy eyes. She looked like she was about to break into tears – hopefully, of joy. Jim still wasn't so sure.

"Josie, I think we better take you inside and have you sit down. Do you feel dizzy or anything?"

The two walked into the kitchen and sat at the table. Jim retrieved a glass from the cabinet and poured her a glass of water. "Here, drink this," Jim said as he handed her the water and added, "Did something happen to your granddaughter? Is she okay?"

Josie nodded, still smiling. Each time she tried to speak, nothing came out. She raised her right index finger and shook it into the air several times as if to say, *'hang on a minute and I'll be okay'*. The words finally came. "She's fine, she's fine. This is good news. This is wonderful, just wonderful! What I've been trying to say is that Shelby and I had a talk about past life experiences. I told her what I remembered about some of mine and how there are people in this life that are carryovers from the past and that we are given a chance to resolve, or continue, those relationships this time around."

"Josie, you're not making any sense. Why are you saying it's wonderful and talking about past lives in the next breath? Are you okay?"

"I wish you would quit asking me that," she said, now slightly irritated. "Oh, I'm sorry, I'm not mad at you. I'm just frustrated that I just can't get the words I want to use out of my mouth the way I want to. I'm too excited."

"Okay... take a deep breath and don't worry about talking right now. Just relax and breathe."

Jose nodded and did exactly as Jim had recommended. Jim saw Josie's shoulders lower slightly as she finally let go of the tension that had built up from her excitement.

"I don't think you've ever seen me like this. I was this excited...or speechless, for that matter," she stated calmly, a bit embarrassed with herself.

Jim faced Josie directly and put his hands on her, reassuring her. She nodded, this time saying, "I'll be okay. As I was trying to say before, Shelby shared with me that she had always felt as if she was missing something in her life. Remember the first time we went flying? I told you that you had flown before and you had probably been a fly boy in WWII."

"If I remember correctly, you also put the plane into a stall and spin to prove your point."

"It worked, didn't it?"

"Point taken," Jim said, nodding his head as he smiled, "But what does that have to do with your granddaughter feeling something was missing in her life?"

Josie continued, "She met some nice guys along the way, but they just never seemed to be the right one for her. At the time, she chalked it up to being focused on getting good grades, finishing med school and then getting through the long hours of her residency. Eventually, she realized it was more than that. Long story short, we did a past-life regression for her."

"What's that?" Jim asked

"It's a process of bringing things from our subconscious, including past time-lines into our consciousness. Anyway, we found she's been waiting for a guy from her past... Past; as in 'past-life.' She told me she had a hunch she may have had a near encounter with him this past spring but didn't know how to approach him. She wasn't sure how she could introduce herself to him, short of walking up and starting a conversation."

"Why didn't she just do that?" Jim asked.

"Oh, she can be a shy little shit sometimes. Having an M.D. behind her name doesn't boost her self confidence when it comes to things like that. She's always been that way; a spitfire most of the time and yet so bashful when it comes to personal matters.

I told her to call out to him and have the Powers-that-Be bring him to her doorstep." Josie paused again, still in shock. She looked at Jim again and said, "Isn't this wonderful?"

"I'm not following you, Josie; what's so wonderful?"

Josie looked into Jim's eyes and said, "That you're here!"

It took a moment for Jim to realize what Josie was inferring. He looked at her in amazement as he shook his head in disbelief.

"Are you saying what I think you're trying so hard to say?"

Josie smiled and nodded. "I told you that true love was just around the corner for you, didn't I kiddo? And I also told you that if you were supposed to meet my granddaughter, you would."

"You're saying I'm supposed to meet you granddaughter? Is this for real?" Jim asked. The past-life concept still was not concrete in his mind.

It was at that instant Josie's granddaughter walked through the door and into the kitchen, already asking, "Nonna, who are you talking to?" Her voice trailed off as Jim and Shelby both did a double-take, looked into each others' eyes in disbelief and in stereo said, "It's you!" Neither could speak. Jim had found his strawberry blonde and Shelby her fly boy.

They both looked at Josie and again in stereo asked, "Did you know?"

She shook her head, "I wish I could say I did. Do you really think I'd be acting like a blubbing idiot like I am, if I had known?" she said with a laugh. "Now come here, both of you, and give me a hug. Oh boy, this is a wonderful day!"

The three stood there for a minute clutching each other tightly. Jim finally spoke first saying, "I don't want to let go because I'm afraid this is just a dream."

Josie responded with, "I guarantee this is as real as it gets."

Jim looked at Shelby. "You know, Josie mentioned that she had a granddaughter several times in passing and I never in my wildest dreams, thought it could be you."

Shelby laughed. "It's strange hearing you call her Josie; she's my 'Nonna'. I've heard all her stories about her favorite fly boy, Jim, but I never expected him and you to be one and the same."

There was a silence again as they stared into each others' eyes. "Is this really true?" Shelby asked.

"That's exactly what I just asked Josie before you came into the room. And to answer your question, I think so... at least I hope so," Jim said.

"Oh yes, this is all for real this time," Josie said. "I think I'll go for a walk and leave you two alone to talk about things."

"No – stay, Nonna. You don't have to leave," Shelby said.

Jim added, "You're part of the reason we've found each other."

"Yes, I do have to leave...I'll be back after a good walk. We will have plenty of time to chat. That I know for sure," Josie said as she put on her floppy straw hat. She grabbed her walking stick and sunglasses, and disappeared out the door.

Jim and Shelby sat staring at each other. Jim shook his head slightly in disbelief.

Shelby looked at Jim puzzled, "What's wrong?"

"Absolutely nothing! I wasn't expecting any of this to happen today."

"Are you disappointed?" Shelby said with a grin.

Disappointed...Are you kidding me? NO! Surprised, shocked, bewildered, and every other synonym you can find in the Thesaurus, but disappointed....no way. I've had so many things happen to me in the last few months, you'd think I couldn't be surprised by anything, but I am," Jim said and then quickly asked, "You are real, aren't you? I mean, I've seen you in my dreams and briefly at the drop zone, but to be honest, I had come to think of you as more of a fantasy than real."

Shelby took Jim's hand and held it to her chest, just above her heart. "What do you feel?"

Jim grinned, "Aroused."

Shelby laughed as she squeezed his hand which was still over her heart. "That's good to know, but the point I was attempting to make was you could feel my heart beating." Shelby paused. "Just a hunch, but you're not much of a romantic, are you?"

"I haven't had much opportunity to practice in recent past. I've been alone for a long time." Jim looked deep into Shelby's eyes. "Do you think this possible past-life connection thing is the real reason we have this attraction and feel the way we do, or is it just an great excuse for having the 'hots' for each other?" Jim asked. "Wait...you do have the 'hots' for me too, right? At least I hope you do."

Shelby smiled, "I assure you, I do."

"Good to know. It would be rather foolish to plan a future together if you didn't plan on being there to participate," Jim said with a wink.

"Participate? Is that what you're going to call it? Trust me, I plan on participating!!

Jim, we share a dream.... I don't see how that could be done without us having shared a past. But I'll settle for 'hot' for each other, if it's what you want to believe."

"To tell you the truth, I hope it's both. Hot for each other and past-life romance. The redundancy might just help give us a head start in getting to know each other."

Shelby just smiled.

"Question for you," Jim said. "When Rabina and I had our little 'incident' at the drop-zone a few weeks ago, you were the first person I remember seeing after I regained consciousness."

Shelby smiled. "So, what's your question?"

"I'm not quite sure..." Jim answered. "I guess my question is, why didn't you stick around?"

"At that point I knew you were going to be okay and help was on the way, but the reaction of the crowd scared me. I thought it best to leave you to the EMT's. Besides, I didn't know if you had something going with your friend Rabina, and if you did, I didn't want to interfere.

I did go to the hospital, though, and waited for you to show up there. I figured you would eventually head in that direction. My thinking was, I'd have a great excuse to check you over and find out more about you. I never thought, but should have known you were a 'guy' and you wouldn't go to the hospital first. You probably figured you could just walk it off, or rubbed dirt on it or something, didn't you?" Shelby asked rhetorically as she rolled her eyes. "Where did you end up going?"

"I don't think you really want to know."

"Yes, I do," Shelby answered

"Um, well, Rabina and I went to my place and grilled some steaks," Jim mumbled, a bit sheepishly.

"WHAT? You've got to be kidding," Shelby said, shaking her head. "You could have had some serious injuries. Come on Jim, how many people do you know are able to 'bounce' like you did and walk away...and then you don't have the sense to stop for x-rays or at least see a doctor."

Jim smiled and answered her question by saying, "Two."

Confused, Shelby said, "What?"

"You asked how many people I know who are able to 'bounce' and walk away...and my answer to that question is *two*," he said with a grin.

Shelby shook her head in disbelief.

Jim smiled, "Are you going to waste this lifetime picking on me for something you probably knew about me from a lifetime ago? Just think of it as a quirky and, I might add, endearing carryover from a lifetime ago."

"I'm guessing you're going to use that excuse every time I question your sanity, aren't you?" Shelby asked as she continued shaking her head.

"You bet! I was told that a good excuse is one you can use over and over again. I think I'm going to like using this past-life thing when it comes to arguments with you in the future," Jim said with a chuckle.

"Oh, you think so, huh? You keep thinking that way, and there won't *be* a future," Shelby said, pretending to be stern. "But keep in mind I can use the same excuse on you...and then we'll see how endearing you think it is."

Jim got serious for a moment. "If you don't mind, I've got to ask. Why were you at the drop zone that day? I mean, I only saw you out there once before that all summer...trust me, I was watching for you."

Shelby went to speak but hesitated, giving what she was going to say a second thought and finally said, "I was going to say you wouldn't believe me, but I think we are both beyond that point, aren't we?" Shelby said rhetorically and continued. "Actually, I heard a voice." She looked at Jim, waiting for a reaction. Jim shrugged his shoulders as he cocked his head and raised his eyebrows. "I understand. I heard a voice telling me to come here today...glad I listened," Jim said and then smiled.

"So, you *do* know what I mean." Shelby grinned. "Well, as I was saying, I heard a voice. I mean I heard an actual *voice* telling me to go to the drop zone that day...so I went."

Jim nodded, still smiling. "Josie mentioned the two of you did a past-life regression last night. What did you find out? You said we shared a dream. Care to elaborate for me?"

"Nonna and I got into a conversation about past lives last night and I told her I had this odd feeling like I had lived before during World War II, and that my love from that life was somewhere here in this one too."

"What made you think that?" Jim inquired.

"I don't know, just a feeling I guess…no, it was actually more than that, it was a *knowing*." Shelby laughed. "I'm not sure what I knew but something just didn't seem right until I saw you at the drop zone this past spring. I was hoping you would come over and talk to me when I was standing by the picture board over in the corner by the over-head doors. I knew you were watching me and I gave you my best 'come-hither' look, but I guess I'm not good at that sort of thing."

"Is that what that was? I thought you had gas," Jim said jokingly and then added with a serious tone, "I wish I had known. I really wanted to come over but I just didn't feel worthy."

"Not worthy…why would you think that?"

"Have you looked in the mirror? You're gorgeous!"

Shelby gave Jim a coy, almost bashful look, saying only, "I'm glad you think so."

"I'm not alone; everyone thought so."

"Ok, that's enough," she said, now blushing and a bit embarrassed. "When I first saw you that day I swear I saw you dressed in a World War II British pilots' uniform for a brief second, complete with olive drab canvas head gear and goggles, ready to climb into a Spitfire at a moment's notice."

Jim couldn't wait any longer; he leaned forward and kissed Shelby softly. At that instant, they were transported back to the moment she kissed him immediately after he had 'bounced' at the drop-zone, and then to a time when they were young lovers during the German occupation of France. Shelby slowly pulled away and gently cradled Jim's face between her hands. She looked deep into his eyes and asked, "Now do you have any doubt that we had, what you called, a past-life thing?"

Jim looked at Shelby, seeing the woman of his dreams, past and present. He said nothing, but shook his head ever so slightly.

Josie's voice rang out from somewhere out on the back porch, "I hope you kids have clothes on, 'cause I'm coming in." Josie opened the door and stepped over the threshold and stood in the doorway of the kitchen, her face still beaming behind a large pair of sunglasses. "So, are we getting caught up on things? I'm glad that I don't have to throw cold water on the two of you," she said laughing.

"Nonna!" Shelby said, exasperated.

"Why are you just standing there with the door wide open? Come on in and join us. We're just talking about this whole past-life thing."

"Can't just yet," She answered.

"Why not?" Jim asked, puzzled. "Do you have asparagus or something that you need to run out and pick?" he said, joking.

"No, it 'cause I've got someone here I think you'll be interested in seeing," Josie said.

Jim looked at Shelby first, wondering if she knew who Josie was referring to, but Shelby just shrugged her shoulders. He then looked back at Josie, finally saying, "Well, why don't you just bring whoever it is in so we can meet him?"

"Oh, you're no fun. You're going to have to guess."

"Come on Josie, I think I've had enough surprises for one day," Jim pleaded.

Josie responded with, "I'll give you a hint. He's someone from your past." She stepped aside and a figure of a man stepped through the doorway behind her. The man was dressed in an English WWII flight suit. At a glance, Jim saw his twenty-year-old wing-man from World War II, Charlie. A flood of past-life memories poured into his consciousness as if everything which had transpired a lifetime ago, were now new again. Tears welled up in Jim's eyes and began to roll down his cheeks. He now remembered Charlie had put himself in harm's way and sacrificed his own life in an effort to draw fire from the German Luftwaffe onto himself, allowing Jim a chance to limp his wounded plane back behind allied lines. If Charlie hadn't done that, it would have been certain death for Jim. When Jim looked at the man again he realized it was Jonathan standing in the doorway. It all made sense now - Jonathan was the incarnation of his wing-man, Charlie. Jim released his bond from Shelby and quickly moved toward Jonathan, wrapping his arms around him as he buried his face in Jonathan's shoulder. "I'm sorry," Jim said, "I never meant for you to die trying to save me. I'm so, so sorry."

"It's all good," Jonathan said. "It was my choice, not yours. That's what a good wing-man does; protect his squad leader. And because I did, I was given the opportunity to raise myself up to a

195

higher conscious plane." Jonathan paused before finishing his thought. "Just as you will be, for inspiring others through your writing."

Jim looked at Jonathan, then Shelby and finally Josie. They all nodded at him.

"It looks like I have no choice here," Jim said.

Jonathan smiled as he cocked his head, "Did you forget that you choose everything in this life?"

"No, that was merely a figure of speech."

Shelby walked over and placed her hand on Jim's lower back, just above his belt. He felt comfort in her touch and wrapped his arm around her shoulder. It felt right having her nestled up against his chest. Jim looked at all of them a bit puzzled. "You would think that with everything that has happened recently that I'd know what to do next, but this is such a new situation for me... So, where do we go from here?"

Shelby answered, "Anywhere we want to go."

"I think we should start by having you meet Rabina. You'll get a kick outta her... consensus is that she may have been your sister last time around. And from what I gather, she was the 'easy' one." Jim said, amused with his comment.

Shelby smiled, "I'd like that. You're sure there's nothing going on between you two? I don't want to step on any toes if there is."

Jim assured Shelby there had never been anything more than friendship between Rabina and him. They were kindred spirits and more like brother and sister than anything else.

Jim looked at Shelby for a moment, then said, "You know, I've been jotting down notes for as long as I can remember; didn't really know why. I never thought I would turn them into anything someone might want to read, much less learn from. But, I'm beginning to see that is exactly what I need to do now." He looked deep into her eyes and asked, "Do you think you could handle being around someone who has been told his mission is to write?"

"I'll be your number one fan!" She said, as she gave Jim a playful nudge with her hip and squeezed his hand. "I don't care what you do as long as there is plenty of time left for us."

Jim looked over at Josie and Jonathan. They were both smiling contently as a golden glow emanating from all around them. Jim cocked his head slightly, saying, "Jonathan, I've never heard you be this quiet for so long. What's wrong?"

Jonathan shook his head, "Nothing's wrong...in fact, everything is right in the world. Congratulations; you've found your love and remembered why you are here. It's all good and nothing more needs to be said..." He paused, "Except, maybe..."

Jim laughed, "I knew you couldn't just leave it there..."

"You know me so well," Jonathan said, nodding in approval. "I was only going to add, don't forget why you are here. It's easy to do when everything is going your way. Remember what you've learned and know that your lessons aren't over. Always watch for omens and ask yourself; what am I to learn, what are my trade-offs... and what are my rewards?"

Jim nodded, "I do know it's my time; I promise I won't forget. I'm sure you'd let me know if I did. And just as a reminder...whenever you feel the need to bring me coolers full of good cold beer, feel free to do so...as long as it's not in the middle of the night again...'k?"

Jonathan grinned. "I'll keep that in mind, but only if I get to help you drink it."

Jim extended his hand and shook Jonathan's "Thanks for being there and not letting me back away from things."

Jonathan gave Jim a knowing smile and replied, "I wish I could take the credit, but in the big scheme of things, it was you who chose to put me there when you needed the help...and if it wasn't me, it would have been someone else."

Jim nodded and said, "I may have squandered chances in the past and I'll try not to do so again." He took a long looked at Shelby and back at Jonathan, "I know this is going to sound 'corny', but with you looking out for me and her as my new wing-man, how could I do any better?"

Shelby squeezed his hand again as she leaned in and whispered in his ear, "It's all a dream."

Jim looked at her in shock.

She laughed and said, "But dreams do come true!"

About the Author

I grew up as the last of four children; the Caboose, as my mother would say, in your typical mid-western, middle-class, middle-America family. My family moved quite a bit when I was young and by the time I was twelve we finally settled right where we started, in Northern Wisconsin. Even at that early age, I knew that I didn't fit into most social groups and felt there had to be more to life than what was on the surface.

Growing up in a small town, my adolescence and early adult life was somewhat uneventful and yet never typical. Underlying it all was a feeling that there had to be *"something more"*. That feeling, along with a good dose of curiosity, led me to try many different things in my search to satisfy that craving and to find meaning and purpose to my life. After high school, I worked manual labor and semi-skilled jobs in my quest... each of them giving perspective, but none providing the answers that I was seeking.

I worked at those jobs for six years before attending college and earning a degree in Business/Computer Science. I worked as a computer programming for a brief time. It was in college that I met, dated and married a girl that I had previously, over a number of years, 'almost-met' many times. We divorced ten years later; we had no children, but great lessons were learned.

I've always written notes to myself, not knowing why I did so. Most of what I have written comes from my own life experiences. I've jumped out of perfectly good airplanes and gone SCUBA diving in remote locations. I became a private pilot to get past my fear of heights and started my own business because I didn't fit well in the corporate world. I've worked as a photographer, ski instructor, crane operator, welder, wood worker and sculptor. I've built homes, made furniture, created leaded glass windows, all combining form with function, among other things – all in an attempt to satisfy a desire for that "*something*" missing in my life. I feel that I have finally found that outlet for my creative energies through writing.

I currently split my time between Wisconsin and Florida. I live in a rural area north of Green Bay, WI with my mighty dog Buddy, shooting photos as the mood and light strikes, and Longboat Key, Florida, where I walk the beach gathering shells and ideas for writing while photographing and being inspired by the changing tides.

More About the Author

The Author, besides writing, has also established himself as an accomplished photographer, furniture maker, sculptor and craftsman.

He has his work displayed in galleries in Wisconsin as well as Florida.

You can view and appreciate his work, along with the opportunity to purchase some of it for yourself, along with more information about his book at: **www.rigoniworks.com**.